# Microeconomics:

# A Simple Introduction

*Also by K.H. Erickson*

## **Simple Introductions**

Choice Theory
Financial Economics
Game Theory
Game Theory for Business
Investment Appraisal
Microeconomics

# Microeconomics:

# A Simple Introduction

K.H. Erickson

© 2014 K.H. Erickson

All rights reserved.
No part of this publication may be reproduced, stored in or introduced into a retrieval system, or transmitted in any form or by any means, including electronic, mechanical, photocopying, recording or otherwise, without the prior permission of the author.

# Contents

1 Introduction to Microeconomics — 6
2 Market Supply and Demand — 12
3 Elasticity — 21
4 Market Failure — 31
5 Consumer Demand — 38
6 Firm Supply and Costs — 53
7 Factors of Production — 63
8 Market Power and Profit Maximization — 72
9 Perfect and Monopolistic Competition — 79
10 Monopoly — 87
11 Oligopoly — 95
12 Games — 105

# 1 Introduction to Microeconomics

Economics can be separated into two main areas of focus; Macroeconomics and Microeconomics. Microeconomics is the focus of this book, as decisions made by individuals and firms in an economy are explained and analysed.

## *The Basic Economic Problem*

The basic economic problem is that of insatiable wants, far beyond the level of essential human needs, in a world of scarce resources. An individual or firm will be held back by time, information, money, and physical or human capital constraints, while their wants and desires have no limit. As a result choices have to made, and certain wants have to be prioritized over others. A choice is a trade-off, where one thing is gained as something else is substituted and given up, and the highest value alternative given up is called the choice's opportunity cost.

## *Production Possibilities Frontier*

Every firm faces an opportunity cost, and must choose its business specialization. It can either focus on only one good or on several product types at once, but both choices involve an opportunity cost as this diagram suggests for a firm deciding between book and video game production.

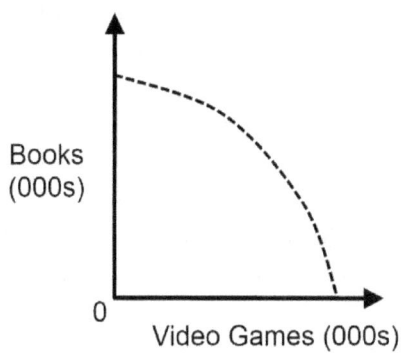

If a firm only produces books and no video games it operates at the leftmost and highest part of the production possibilities frontier (PPF) above, while a choice to only produce video games sees it operate at the rightmost and lowest part of the PPF. A move along the curve from left to right sees the firm switch from only producing books, to mostly producing books but also some video games, to a focus on video games with a minority of books, and finally only producing video games at the rightmost point.

As the firm moves away from book production the PPF's shape changes, becoming steeper as the focus shifts to video games. This represents diminishing returns to production and just like all other resources low cost video game production opportunities may be in limited supply, as it's far harder to find the resources needed for the one hundredth video game than the first when relevant resources haven't yet been used up. Initial units of video game production come at a low opportunity cost, with only a small amount of books required as substitution as shown by the flatter part of the curve. But later units see the production cost rise to give a higher opportunity cost of a large number of books, represented by the steeper curve.

Moving from the rightmost end of the PPF to the left shows that diminishing returns also holds for increasing book production, and the first few units of books come at a low cost as shown by the curve's steepness, but the final units are far more expensive as shown by a flatter curve. Diminishing returns and rising opportunity cost holds for all production, and the graph will apply for all products.

## *Marginal Costs and Benefits*

Producers and consumers make decisions at the margin and assess the effects of an incremental (i.e. one unit) change, determining the marginal cost and marginal benefit of a choice before they proceed. The PPF just explained gives the overall cost relationship between two goods as the amount of each changes, and from this the marginal cost can be found, which represents the cost of producing one more unit measured in terms of the activity foregone. In the example here the marginal cost would give the number of books produced per video game as the amount of video games rises, and diminishing returns to production ensure increasing marginal costs of production.

A consumer with no books or video games can gain significantly from them but the more of each good they have the less satisfaction will be derived from each additional unit. And as the amount of video games consumed rises the number of books an individual will sacrifice for another video game falls, due to these diminishing returns from consumption, and this gives a decreasing marginal benefit, defined as the benefit gained by one more unit of consumption measured in terms of the buyer's willingness to pay. The following graph combines marginal benefits (MB) and marginal costs (MC) to reveal how an individual or firm can make an efficient choice.

The downward sloping MB curve shows the decreasing marginal benefit while the upward sloping MC curve shows the increasing marginal cost, and the point where the two curves cross is the efficient number of video games to select for both a consumer and producing business. With a lower amount chosen the MB curve is greater than the MC curve, and there are still net benefits to be had from more video games. And selecting a higher number of video games than where the two curves cross sees MC exceed MB, and additional units are not worth pursuing as they only bring a net cost. This result will hold far beyond this individual example, and irrespective of the specific details the point where MB equals MC will be best for all consumers and producers.

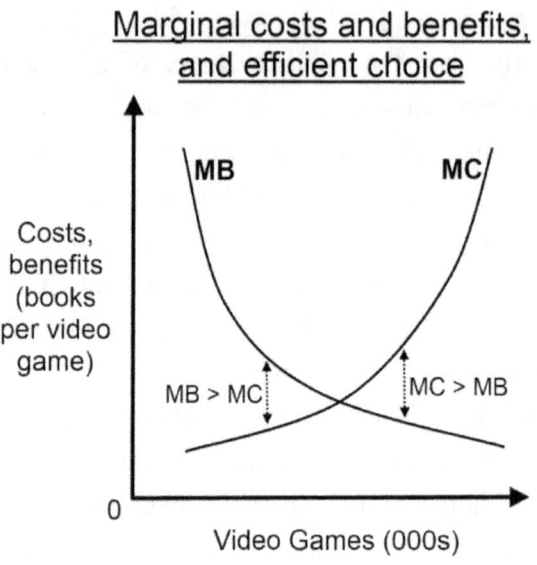

*Topics in Economics*

Opportunity cost and balancing marginal costs with marginal benefits is the foundation for all economics issues, and the point where the two are equal is the stable equilibrium. This is a partial equilibrium if the analysis concerns individual people or markets, and a general equilibrium if it assesses all decision-makers together. Comparative statics compares two or more equilibrium points, while comparative dynamics looks at the path and process of adjustment to a new efficient equilibrium or away from an old one. Microeconomics focuses primarily upon comparative statics and partial equilibrium.

Microeconomics may analyse if people rationally pursue the efficient outcome or if they act in irrational ways due to biases. It's usually assumed that individuals and firms act rationally and follow their incentives, seeking the best possible outcome, but power, information or wealth constraints may get in the way of their goals.

Assessing the behaviours of economic actors will involve data measurement and analysis as economic models are built and predictions tested against the facts, before a theory is developed that allows simplifying generalizations to be made. A model can only test positive statements, those based on what is, and it can't assess normative statements, those based upon personal values and ideas of what should be. But personal values can offer insight as to why an equilibrium solution may remain out of reach, and give suggestions as to how to resolve this.

There are two different systems used to achieve equilibrium outcomes, the first being the public sector planning model characterized by state control and leaders who make rules to ensure the desired results, and the second involving the private sector and free markets where an equilibrium is thought to arise naturally without intervention, due to an 'invisible hand'. The next chapter looks at markets in depth.

# 2 Market Supply and Demand

### *Markets Defined*

A market is simply any arrangement which allows self-interested buyers and sellers to gain information and undertake business transactions, and the system implicitly assumes the existence of privately owned property rights where a buyer will exchange a sum of money to acquire rights over the seller's products. Markets are based around the concept of effective competition and perfect information, to maintain reasonable prices and to ensure that neither side of the interaction gets involved in a deal that doesn't serve their interests, but with market transactions usually covered by law the government may step in and resolve market imperfections if these conditions don't hold.

The last section examined consumers and producers but when it comes to the marketplace it's more useful to use the terms buyers and sellers instead. A market will not necessarily see a direct transaction between those who produce a good and those who consume it, and using the terms buyer and seller accounts for the prevalence of middlemen who make trades on others' behalf.

## The Buyer's Demand Function

Buyers determine the market demand, where the quantity demanded of good 'x' (QDx) is a function (F) of the price of good x (Px), the prices of substitute (Py) or complement goods (Pz), the number of buyers in the market (N), buyers' income (Y), and the utility gained from the item (U) based upon individual preferences. QDx = F (Px, Py, Pz, N, Y, U).

## The Seller's Supply Function

Sellers determine the market supply, where the quantity supplied of good 'x' (QSx) is a function (G) of the price of good x (Px), prices of input goods required for supply (Pi), prices of alternative goods (Pa), the total number of sellers in the market (T), and government regulations affecting barriers to entry into the market for new firms (B). QSx = G (Px, Pi, Pa, T, B).

## Market Efficiency

When the sellers' supply function is combined with the buyers' demand function the efficient market equilibrium is created. The following diagram represents market efficiency, where supply and demand curves cross and where supply and demand are equal.

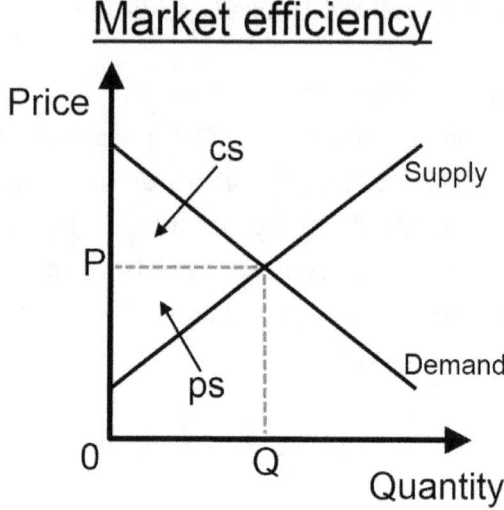

The demand curve slopes downwards as a lower price naturally increases the relative value of the product to raise the quantity of people who will buy it, ensuring a negative correlation between price and the quantity of a good demanded. A price rise will see demand fall due to both an income effect where buyers can't afford the product, and a substitution effect where they turn to alternatives giving better value, while a price reduction will see the opposite.

The supply curve slopes upwards as supplying a higher quantity of goods naturally incurs a greater cost for a seller, ensuring a positive correlation between price and the quantity of a good supplied. A rise in quantity supplied will see prices (i.e. costs) increase for a seller as this requires the investment of more of its limited resources, while lower quantity supplied has the opposite effect.

A stable equilibrium point occurs where the buyers' demand curve and sellers' supply curve cross, with a product price at level P and quantity traded at amount Q, and this efficient market equilibrium offers benefits to both the buyer and seller.

## *Consumer Surplus and Producer Surplus*

Although the buyer would be willing to pay a higher price for the first units of product quantity where marginal benefits per unit are higher the buyer gets a price of P, below his demand curve, and gains the consumer surplus savings based on the area of the triangle labelled 'cs' in the previous diagram. The seller would be willing to accept a lower price for the first units of product quantity where marginal costs per unit are lower but gets price P, above his costs and supply curve, and this offers a producer surplus profit shown by the 'ps' triangle area in the diagram.

## *The Efficient Market Mechanism*

It's worth investigating exactly how the efficient market equilibrium price and quantity comes about, where demand equals supply. The following diagram shows the market mechanism as the price and quantity demanded and supplied are pushed to the efficient equilibrium point.

## The market mechanism

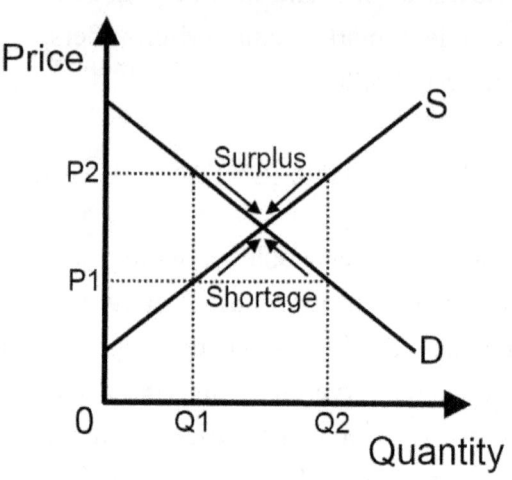

If the price is below the equilibrium level where demand and supply functions cross, for example at price P1, then the corresponding amount of a product supplied, Q1, will be less than the quantity demanded, Q2, creating a shortage. But the market should resolve this problem as those buyers with higher incomes or who value the product more will pay above the market price, to ensure they're one of the few who get the product. This sees the buyer's price rise to the equilibrium, and sellers will see the higher price these buyers are paying for products and raise their supply levels to profit from it, thus ending the shortage and pushing the market to the efficient equilibrium.

If the price is above the efficient point where demand and supply meet, at a price such as P2, the resulting level of product demand, Q1, will be less than quantity supplied, Q2, to create a surplus of excess unwanted stock. But the market should resolve this as suppliers will sell the leftover unwanted stock at discount prices, and the lower prices will see buyers increase their demand quantity to purchase the discounted goods, bringing an end to the stock surplus as the market reaches the equilibrium point.

## *Shifts in the Efficient Equilibrium*

So far only the effects of changes in a product's price have been examined, but as the demand and supply functions earlier highlighted there are other factors that determine the quantity of a product's demand; QDx = F (Px, Py, Pz, N, Y, U), or supply; QSx = G (Px, Pi, Pa, T, B). While changes in a product's price (Px) cause movements along the demand or supply curve as just explained, all of the remaining factors shift either the demand curve or the supply curve. The curves may shift left (same thing as a demand curve downward shift or a supply curve upward shift), or right (same thing as a demand curve upward shift or a supply curve downward shift). These shifts create a new efficient equilibrium in the market.

## *Shifts in the Demand Curve*

The following diagram looks into the effects of an increase in buyers' income (Y) which will shift the demand curve right (i.e. up), ceteris paribus (other things being equal). It's worth noting that the effect would be the same with a rise in the price of substitute goods (Py) or number of buyers in the market (N), a decrease in the price of complementary products (Pz), or a change in preferences (U) that sees buyers like the product more.

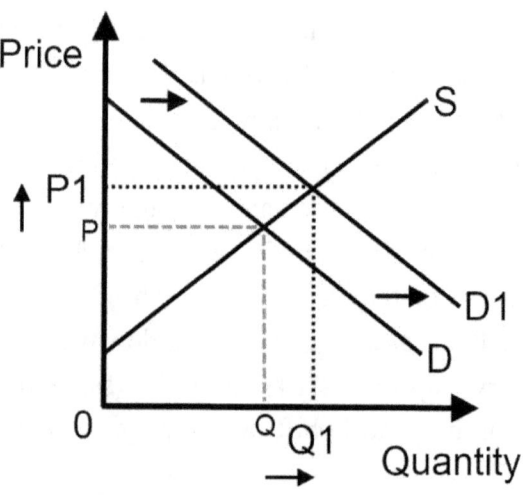

Increasing buyer income gives a product a higher relative value and increases demand at every price level, shifting the demand curve right from D to D1. This sees the old equilibrium price now linked with a higher quantity of demand where demand is greater than supply. The market will treat this as the shortage scenario explained earlier, with buyers raising the price they're willing to pay to create a new equilibrium point with a higher price, P1, and a higher quantity of demand, Q1, than the previous equilibrium. And in the opposite scenario where demand decreases the curve shifts to the left (i.e. down) and the reverse situation plays out.

## *Shifts in the Supply Curve*

The next diagram examines the effects of a rightward shift in the supply curve (i.e. downward) caused by a reduction in the price of resources used as inputs (Pi). This has the same effect as an increase in the price of alternative products (Pa), increased barriers to market entry (B), or a reduction in the total number of sellers in the market (T). A reduction in the price of supply inputs makes selling more profitable and shifts the supply curve right from S to S1, increasing product supply at every price level. The old equilibrium price of P is now linked with higher supply where supply exceeds demand for surplus stock. This sees sellers reduce their product's price to shift the stock to create a new equilibrium at P1 with quantity Q1, with a higher quantity of product units being traded than the original equilibrium but at a lower price.

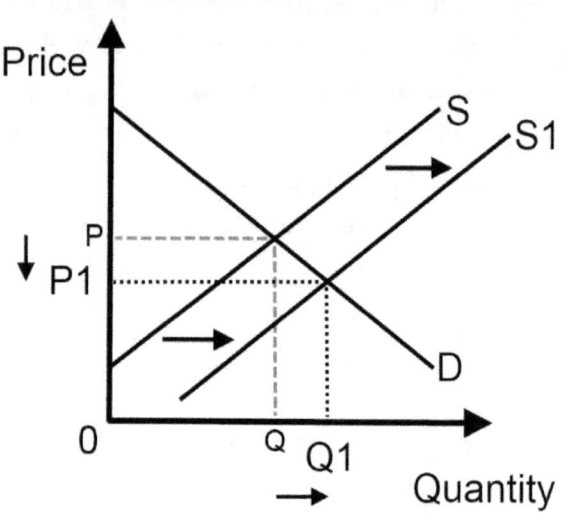

And in the opposite situation where supply decreases the curve shifts to the left (i.e. up), and a similar process occurs but in the opposite direction, as the stock surplus scenario is replaced with a shortage that the market can resolve.

# 3 Elasticity

The last section examined how changes in a product's price affect the quantity demanded or supplied and vice versa, but it's not enough to know that a change in price will push the level of demand or supply up or down. To be able to make use of this information we must know the scale of the market response to a price change.

Elasticity (El) measures the percentage (%) change ($\Delta$) in a dependent variable given a proportionate change in the independent variable, and if Y is used to denote a dependent variable and X an independent variable:

$$El = \% \Delta \text{ in } Y / \% \Delta \text{ in } X$$
$$= (\Delta Y / Y) / (\Delta X / X)$$
$$= (X / Y) \times (\Delta Y / \Delta X)$$

## *Price Elasticity of Demand*

From a seller's point of view the dependent variable is the quantity of his products demanded by buyers, and looking at the demand function; $QDx = F(Px, Py, Pz, N, Y, U)$, the only independent variable that a seller can influence directly is the price of his product (Px), with all other factors beyond his control. A seller will therefore be interested in how changing a product's price affects its demand, to determine if he can get away with charging a higher price or if a price cut would be rewarded with greater profits. The (own) price elasticity of demand (PED) will almost certainly be negative due to the inverse relationship between a good's price and its demand, and it represents the percentage change in quantity demanded as a response to a percentage change in the good's price:

$$PED = \% \Delta \text{ in quantity demanded (QD)} / \% \Delta \text{ in product price (P)}$$
$$= (\Delta QD / QD) / (\Delta P / P)$$
$$= (P / QD) \times (\Delta QD / \Delta P)$$

## *Changing Price Elasticity of Demand*

The following diagram shows a typical downward sloping linear demand curve, and how elasticity varies depending on the point of assessment.

The values of price (P) and demand quantity (Q) are key factors in the elasticity formula, and when each equals zero at the respective axis elasticity takes on an extreme value. If price equals zero then the price elasticity of demand formula, $PED = (P / QD) \times (\Delta QD / \Delta P)$, gives the numerator in the first part of the equation this value to make elasticity overall equal zero (El = 0). An elasticity of zero represents perfectly inelastic demand, where a change in price has no effect on the quantity demanded.

## Price elasticity of demand

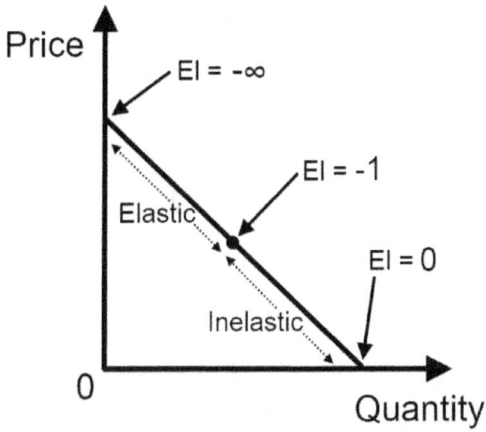

If the demand quantity equals zero the denominator in the first part of the equation above will equal zero, and although dividing by zero leaves this and the overall equation undefined, as the quantity approaches zero the elasticity will become greater and tend toward negative (as the demand slope is negative) infinity. This situation is labelled as El = - ∞ in the diagram to represent perfectly elastic demand, and at this point any change in price will have a limitless effect on quantity demanded.

In a situation where the price, P, and demand quantity, QD, are identical the price elasticity of demand equation will simplify to see the change in demand quantity equal the change in price. This represents unit elasticity, and occurs in the diagram where El = -1 in the middle of the demand curve. Between this point and the point where QD equals 0 and El = - ∞ (or approaches it to be more accurate) the price elasticity of demand curve is elastic, and between the unit elasticity point and the point where P equals 0 and El = 0 the demand curve is inelastic.

## *Point and Arc Elasticity Measurement*

The results of the price elasticity of demand calculation just mentioned, PED = (P / QD) x (ΔQD / ΔP), may be inaccurate due to the uncertainty over which values of P and QD to use in the elasticity formula above. Either the original values before the percentage change could be used or those reached after the change, and each set of values will give a different PED result. There are two popular solutions to get around this problem, and the first method uses point elasticity to find the PED at a single point instead of over the area of change. This replaces the change in a variable, ΔQD and ΔP, with its partial derivative, dQD and dP:

$$\text{Point elasticity} = (dQD / QD) / (dP / P)$$
$$= (P / QD) \times (dQD / dP)$$

The arc method is the second way to get around the uncertainty of whether to use start or post percentage change values of P and Q in the PED formula. This method simply takes the start values (denoted as 1) and end values (denoted as 2) of P and Q, and then averages them to find the middle point to be used in the formula:

$$\text{Arc elasticity} = ([(P1 + P2) / 2] / [(QD1 + QD2) / 2]) \times (\Delta QD / \Delta P)$$

However, the arc elasticity method assumes that the part of the demand curve between start and end points is linear. Therefore the greater the curvature actually is in reality the less accurate the arc elasticity result will be.

Both the point and arc elasticity measures can give a seller an approximation of the effect changes in their product's price has upon buyer demand, but the elasticity may have to be calculated multiple times as it may change constantly with a movement down the demand curve.

## *Constant Elasticities*

An elastic curve means that a price movement sees an exaggerated change in the quantity demanded, while an inelastic curve gives an understated change in quantity demanded. This means that when prices are high (linked with elastic demand) a firm should lower prices, to see a rise in demand greater than the price cut and increase the value of P x Q for greater total revenue and profits. But a price rise should be avoided with elastic demand as this reduces profits. And if prices are low (giving inelastic demand) a firm should raise prices, as the fall in demand will be lower than the increase in price, for a greater P x Q value for higher total revenue and profits. But a price cut should be avoided in this situation as it will reduce profits.

The changing elasticity for a linear demand curve puts constraints on a supplier, as prices can never be raised too high without sacrificing profits. A far better situation for a supplier is to find a product with a constant inelastic demand like that given in curve D1 below, and then prices could be raised without losing buyer demand and revenue. A situation to avoid is one approaching D2 with constant elastic demand, and in this case any price rise takes away demand and profits. Curve D3 shows constant unit elasticity, as sales and revenue are steady and predictable.

## Constant elasticities

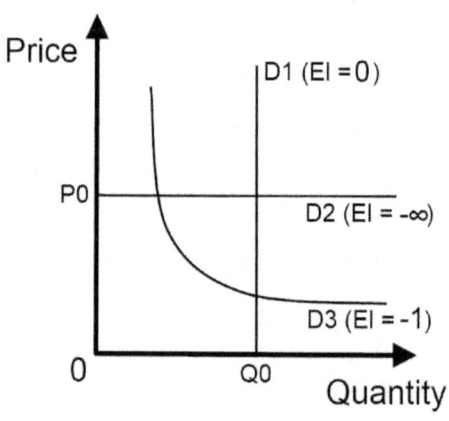

## Causes of Inelastic Demand

Factors reducing the price elasticity of demand, as a seller/producer would want, include a lack of substitute goods, high priced substitute products, advertising that builds the product's reputation, and a high buyer income. Additional factors to increase product inelasticity are to select a product type that's a necessity and routine or addictive as opposed to being a one-off luxury purchase, a more durable type of good, and a product involving a short-run impulsive buy which doesn't allow a proper longer-run assessment before purchase.

## Cross Price Elasticity of Demand

Some of the factors affecting a product's (own) price elasticity of demand can be examined in depth, and the cross-price elasticity of demand examines how a product's demand quantity (QDx) is affected by a change in the price of a different product (Pz):

$$\text{Cross-price elasticity} = \frac{\% \Delta \text{ in demand of good x (QDx)}}{\% \Delta \text{ in price of good z (Pz)}}$$
$$= (Pz / QDx) \times (\Delta QDx / \Delta Pz)$$

The cross-price elasticity may be either positive or negative, and it will typically be positive if the two goods being analyzed are substitutes (e.g. beer and cider), and will typically be negative if the two goods involved are complements (e.g. bread and butter).

## *Income Elasticity of Demand*

Income elasticity of demand gives the change in a product's demand following a change in buyer income:

Income elasticity = % $\Delta$ in quantity demanded (QD) / % $\Delta$ in income (Y)
= (Y / QD) x ($\Delta$QD / $\Delta$Y)

The income elasticity of demand is determined by the level of buyer income and the type of good involved. A normal good has positive income elasticity, with a rise in buyer income linked with greater demand. But an inferior good has negative income elasticity, with a rise in income causing buyers to reduce their demand for the product and replace it with demand for superior goods instead.

## *Price Elasticity of Supply*

Like demand, s product's quantity of supply will be affected by its price. The price elasticity of supply (PES) represents the percentage change in quantity supplied as a response to a percentage change in the good's price:

$$PES = \% \Delta \text{ in quantity supplied (QS)} /$$
$$\% \Delta \text{ in product price (P)}$$
$$= (P / QS) \times (\Delta QS / \Delta P)$$

The (own) price elasticity of supply will usually be positive, due to the positive correlation between a good's price and the amount a seller will supply. The level of the price elasticity of supply will depend upon the excess capacity that a firm possesses and the time period in question, with longer periods linked with more elastic supply. In the following diagram a firm's supply curve is shown for three different time periods, as Si represents the immediate supply, Ss gives short-run supply, and Sl shows the longer-run supply.

## Price elasticity of supply

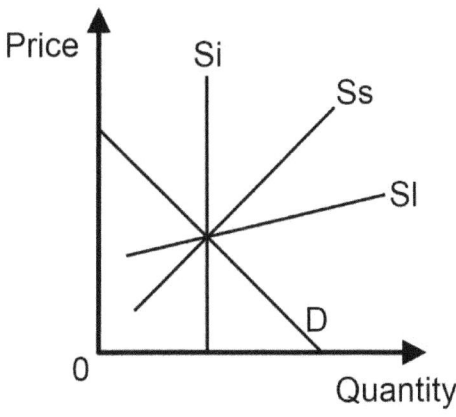

In the immediate time period a firm is unable to react to any changes in the market price for its products, as this process will naturally take time. This keeps immediate supply (Si) perfectly inelastic with regard to price, and changes in the market price will not see any change in supply. In the short-run a firm can adjust some of the factors of production (e.g. hire more workers) to enable it to partially adjust supply to any market price changes, and this makes short-run supply (Ss) relatively elastic as the diagram shows. In the long-run a firm can adjust all of the factors of production to change its supply with the market price, as it will have time to invest in excess capacity such as new factories or buildings, and improve its product development and distribution channels. This gives a flatter and highly elastic long-run supply curve (Sl), which makes the firm more flexible and able to deal with any challenges presented by the market.

# 4 Market Failure

*Government Intervention, with Minimum Prices*

Despite the effectiveness with which markets may be capable of self-correcting to bring about an equilibrium outcome, government may still decide to intervene in situations where they believe the market won't bring about the desired result. The diagram below examines a situation where a government sets a minimum price for the market, and the consequences that may follow.

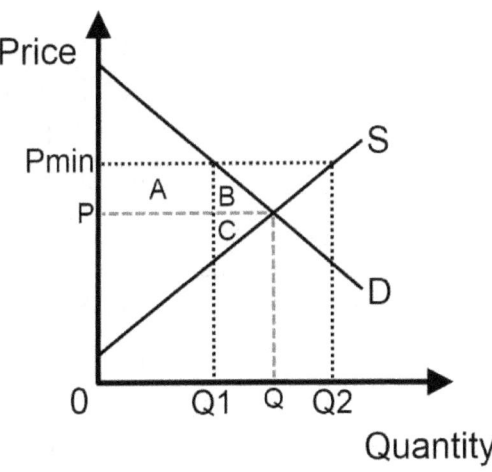

This minimum price (Pmin) might be set for firms, if a government wants to protect the nation's businesses from being undercut by low cost foreign imports, or it could be set for individuals, in terms of a minimum wage to protect citizens from being underpaid and exploited. While the natural equilibrium will be where supply and demand curves cross with a price of P and quantity at level Q, the state's desire to protect people or businesses sees them set a higher minimum price at Pmin instead, which keeps the optimal market quantity Q out of reach.

## *Deadweight Loss for Society*

The minimum price will create a deadweight loss as it removes the consumer surplus given by the B triangle and the producer surplus of the C triangle. It also transfers profits from consumers (buyers or employers) to producers (firms or workers) to the value of rectangle A. This is the excess of the minimum price over the market equilibrium, Pmin - P, multiplied by the lowest quantity the minimum price will bring about, Q1, where price meets demand.

However, if producers of goods or work don't adapt to the impact the minimum price has on the market then the deadweight loss can be even worse, as they may naturally supply a quantity of resources linked with the supply curve for that price to give a long-run outcome of price Pmin and quantity Q2. This would see a surplus supply of level Q2 -

Q1, which represents wasted stock for product supply or unemployment if workers were involved. The government could only hope that in time the market would adjust, to see the demand curve shift right to create a new stable equilibrium where supply equals demand at price Pmin and quantity Q2.

## *Government Intervention, with Supply Restrictions*

State intervention can cause problems even if it doesn't directly set a minimum price, and forcing a certain level of supply on society can cause a similar result. The following diagram shows a scenario where the government puts restrictions on supply, perhaps limiting the sale of alcohol to avoid related social problems, or putting limits on the number of taxi licenses they offer to reduce the negative impact motor vehicle traffic has on nearby residents.

The natural market equilibrium is at price P and quantity Q as before, but this is now prevented by the supply restriction which ensures that the market supply quantity can't rise above level Q1. This law essentially creates a new supply curve representing maximum supply, Smax, and with the demand curve unable to cross the original supply curve the new equilibrium becomes the point where it crosses the new supply curve, giving an outcome of price Ps and quantity Q1. Overall, consumers suffer - (A + B), producers gain A - C, and the wider economy loses B + C and sees area A change hands. Overall there is a deadweight loss for society of the size of area A + B.

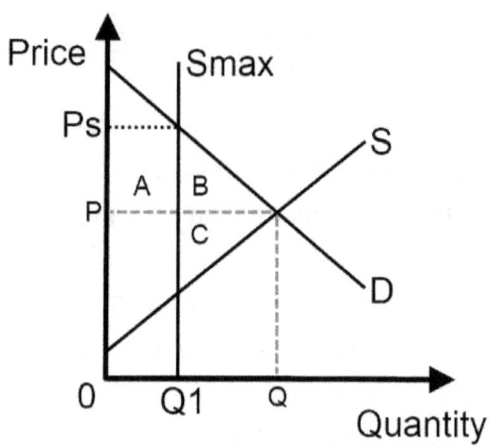

*Asymmetric Information*

Government attempts to resolve what they see as market failure may come with good intentions but their actions can potentially ruin the market equilibrium and bring about an inefficient outcome. However, at times there may be good cause for government intervention, and without it buyers or sellers may be victimized. Markets can work well with frequent transactions between buyers and sellers, and limited resources involved in an exchange, but with infrequent transactions and large amounts of resources exchanged one party may lack complete knowledge and this gives the other side the advantage of asymmetrical information. And this is a situation the more informed buyer or seller is likely to exploit.

Adverse selection is the process where an undesirable collection of buyers or sellers possess greater information than those they hope to trade with, and are more likely to take part in a market exchange than desirable buyers or sellers as they forecast high potential returns. Typically the rogue element will be sellers, and they create a situation where there are two types of seller in the market; high quality sellers offering a good service and low quality sellers giving a poor service.

A buyer will pay a high price for a good quality service but only a low price for a low quality service, yet a buyer can't be sure which sellers offer which as all will naturally insist that they are high quality sellers, with only the sellers holding the asymmetric information and knowing for sure. With buyers unable to separate the good sellers from the bad a buyer must judge them as one group, and will be willing to pay a certain price accordingly. A buyer will pay a price below the high price a guaranteed good seller would get, to account for the risk of a poor service, but above the low price a certain poor seller would get, to account for the potential gain of a good service.

The moderate price a buyer will pay for a service of unknown quality is less than what a high quality service is worth, and as a result good sellers are likely to remove themselves from the market place. But the moderate price is above what poor sellers giving a low quality service are worth, and this attracts them to the market in large number. These two factors create the adverse selection scenario where buyers can't get a high quality service.

In situations where asymmetric information is endemic, such as when dealing with complex products and where businesses can't fully reassure buyers, legislation may be needed to protect consumers from potentially opportunistic firms. The problems in the financial industry have shown that markets can't always be relied upon to be efficient, and government may still have a big role to play in an economy. But then again there's nothing to stop government from abusing their power just as a business might.

## *Moral Hazard*

Moral hazard is another example of market failure between buyer and seller, an ex post (after the fact) contractual issue that can arise if one side has information that allows them to act opportunistically after the transaction has begun. A seller may deliver a good service during initial contact with a buyer, but once a contract and a deposit has been secured the seller may feel they no longer need to be on their best behaviour, and may then offer a substandard service and act dishonestly. Buyers can also be responsible for moral hazard and may agree to pay in instalments for a product they know they can't afford, leaving the seller without full payment for a product.

There are various ways for a business to signal high quality and reassure buyers, such as openly investing in premium resources for a high quality service, building a trusted brand, or giving contracts, warrantees or insurance. Trade association memberships are a form of self regulation that sellers can get involved with, but this may lack meaning to buyers if it is commonplace, and there's the risk that a type of cartel may result. Even if sellers start with good intentions self-regulation comes with screening costs that may change their minds in practice.

# 5 Consumer Demand

Earlier analysis has examined the market as a whole but investigating market participants in depth will reveal the factors driving supply and demand. Consumers determine the demand side of the market and this is based around the utility (pleasure or need fulfilment) that they gain from economic activity, with a consumer thought to attempt to maximize their utility given their budget constraints.

### *Budget Constraint*

Consumption levels will be limited by a consumer's disposable income, and this 'budget constraint' restricts an individual's capacity to maximize utility.

The following diagram revisits the example at the start of the book involving two goods; books and video games. But instead of seeing things from the producer's supply side the focus is now on a consumer's demand side. In this theoretical example the price of the goods and the limited income of a consumer here mean that a maximum of ten books could be bought if all disposable income was put toward books, while the higher price of video games only allow five to be bought if all income went there instead. These points are joined by the budget constraint line which shows the alternative affordable consumption options available to a consumer that spends all of their income, and point A represents consumption of mostly books with few video games. The slope of the budget line = - Pb / Pvg, where Pb is the price of books and Pvg the price of video games.

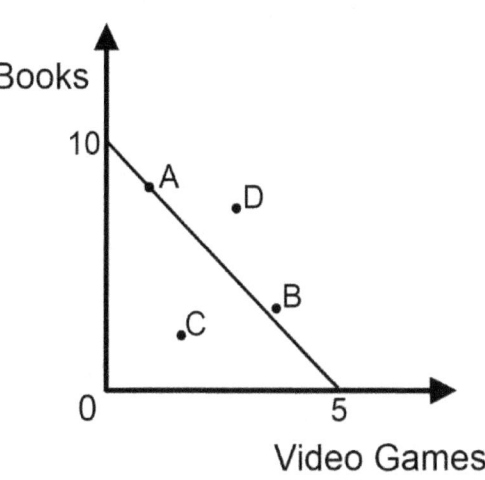

## The budget constraint

A consumer doesn't have to indulge in the maximum possible consumption represented by a place on the budget line, and any point within this line is also an option. One possibility is point C, as a consumer buys both books and video games but doesn't spend their remaining income.

Point B and D lie beyond the budget constraint line here and are therefore currently unaffordable to a consumer, no matter how they choose to allocate their income. For point B or D to be available to a consumer either their income will have to rise or the price of one or both goods must fall, to see a point move within a new budget line. If a consumer's income increased the budget line will shift outwards (up-right) in a parallel move to show the new maximum affordable consumption level, and the reverse shift will occur with decreased income. If a good's price fell the budget line will pivot outwards for that good, to show the maximum affordable at the new price using all income, and a price rise will see a pivot inward.

## *Indifference Curves*

While the budget constraint line shows the consumption a consumer could select, what they actually would select depends upon which option offers the most utility. It's assumed that consumers naturally prefer a greater quantity of one good to less of it, but the choice when faced with a trade-off between books or video games is determined by their unique preferences, and these are usually represented using preference curves known as indifference curves. The following diagram shows some theoretical indifference curves for a consumer, with various points highlighted on them to represent different combinations of video games and books.

# Consumer preferences and indifference curves

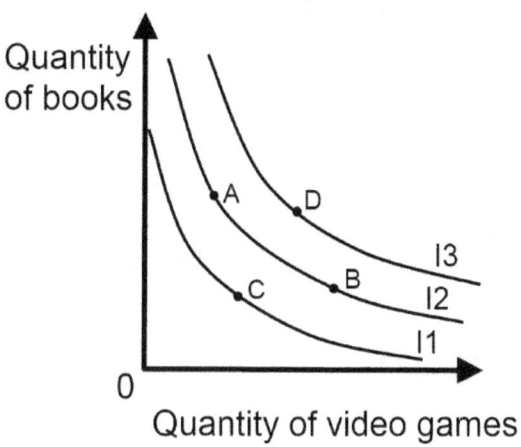

I1, I2, and I3 in the above diagram are three different indifference curves, and each shows various combinations of books and video games for which a consumer is indifferent (unchanging utility), but a higher curve is preferred to a lower one as more books or video games is better than less and offers greater utility. The consumer will be indifferent between bundle of goods A (which has more books than video games) and bundle B (which has more video games than books) as both lie on indifference curve I2, and both of these bundles are preferred to bundle C which lies on lower curve I1 and gives less of each good. And the most preferred bundle of goods labelled here is bundle D as that sits on highest indifference curve I3 with more of both books and video games.

## *Marginal Rate of Substitution*

The slope at any point of an indifference curve gives the marginal rate of substitution (MRS) for the goods, and the $MRS_{(B \text{ to } VG)}$ here $= - \Delta B / \Delta VG$, where $\Delta B$ represents the change in books and $\Delta VG$ the change in video games.

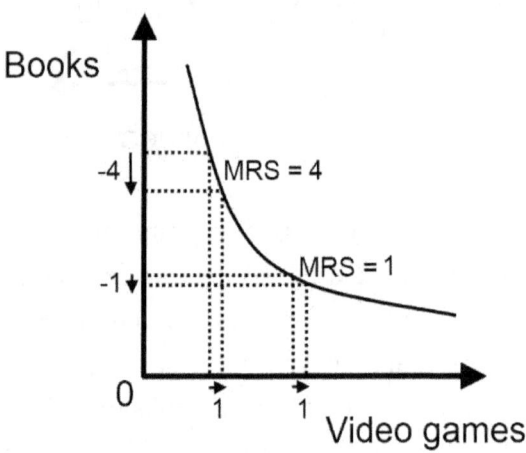

In this indifference curve the marginal rate of substitution (MRS) starts out high, and four books will be substituted and given up to gain just one video game:

$$MRS_{(B \text{ to } VG)} = - \Delta B / \Delta VG$$
$$= - (-4) / 1$$
$$= 4$$

Moving down the indifference curve reduces the MRS of books for video games, and soon enough only one book will be substituted for one video game, $MRS_{(B \text{ to } VG)} = -(-1)/1 = 1$. The reduction of the $MRS_{(B \text{ to } VG)}$ can be explained with the idea of diminishing returns explained earlier. Moving down the curve represents a switch from a high amount of books and few video games, where video games have a high relative value as additional books offer limited gains, to having few books and a high amount of video games, with a lower relative video game value.

While the MRS reveals how many units of a good an individual will exchange for a unit of another, the marginal utility (MU) is the change in utility as a good's quantity changes by one unit, holding other factors constant. Marginal utility can be found by performing mathematical differentiation on a consumer's utility function (i.e. total utility), and it divides the change in the total utility (TU) given by a good by the change in the quantity of that good, e.g. for books $MU = \Delta TU / \Delta B$. The ratio of one good's MU to the other good's MU is another way to find the marginal rate of substitution (MRS).

## *Types of Indifferences Curves*

Although the curved out north-east indifference curve just examined is the most common indifference curve shape there are exceptions, and the MRS will not always follow the same trend as the previous example with books and video games. If the goods involved were perfect substitutes the marginal rate of substitution will remain constant throughout and the indifference curves will be straight lines. In this case there will never be a point where diminishing returns set in for one good relative to another, as it never offered superior returns in the first place.

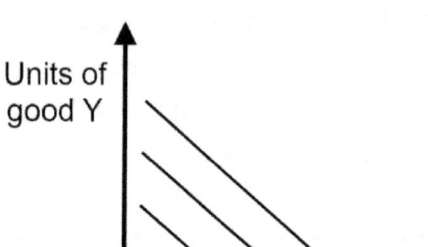

If goods are perfect complements then there won't be a MRS at all, and there's no way to substitute between the products. The only way to move to a more preferred higher indifference curve (from I1 to I2, or I2 to I3) will be to increase the quantity of both goods together.

On some occasions indifference curves may take on a more unusual pattern, breaking the assumption that more of a good is preferred to less. One good may give disutility to a consumer (e.g. nuts for a consumer with a nut allergy), and in this situation a consumer will gain greater utility and move to a more preferred higher indifference curve (from I1 to I2 to I3) by consuming less of that good.

## Perfect complement goods

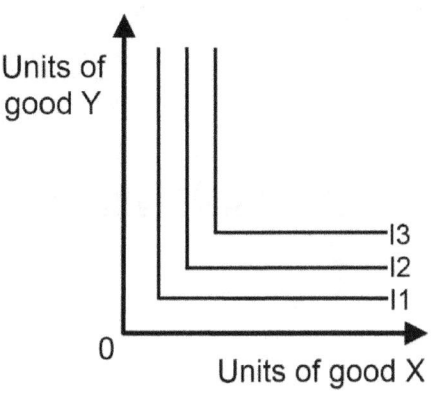

## A good giving disutility

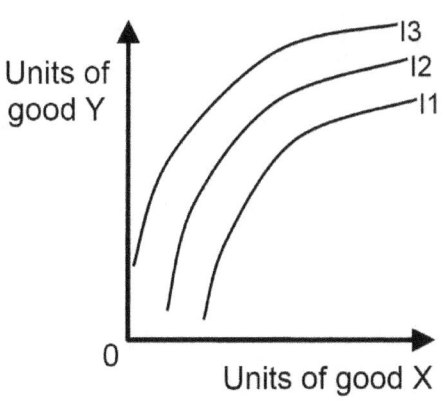

It's also possible for a product to be both good (giving utility) and bad (giving disutility) for an individual, as very specific preferences see indifference curves closed around a 'bliss point' with a certain combination of goods, and a move away from this point reduces utility (e.g. a dose of essential medicine). In this next diagram the bliss point offers the highest utility, any point on curve I3 offers less utility, a point on further away curve I2 offers less still, and any point on curve I1 offers even less utility.

## Preferences closed around bliss point

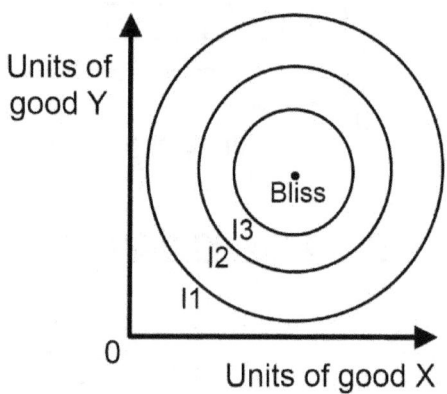

*Equilibrium in Consumption*

Once an individual's preferences and their budget line are both known the next step is to combine the two to find the consumption equilibrium, and this shows how a consumer will maximize utility given their financial resource constraints.

The selected point to maximize utility will be point A in the following diagram, where the dashed budget line is tangent to the highest available indifference curve I2. Point E is also available with this budget line, but it won't be selected as it offers lower utility being on lower indifference curve I1.

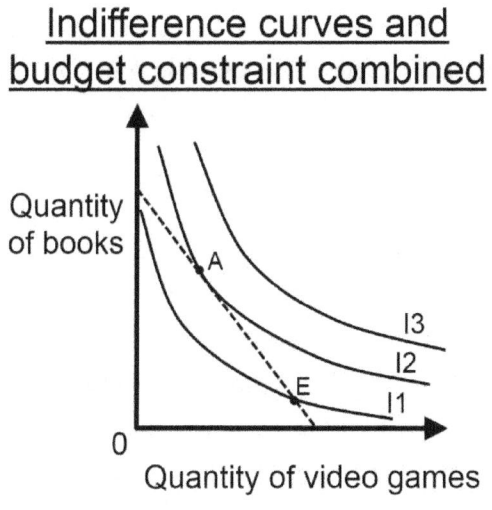

Point A in the diagram can be used to give a part of an Engel curve, which gives the relationship between income and consumption, as the budget line is given for a certain level of income and point A gives the associated consumption of books and video games. To find the remaining points and form a complete Engel curve for a good alternative income levels can also be assessed, and this would see the budget constraint shift in or out in parallel and the place where it cut the highest indifference curve can give another point on an Engel curve.

And point A above may also be used to give a part of a demand curve, as it shows the consumption (i.e. demand) of books and video games at their current prices. A complete demand curve could be formed by assessing other prices for the goods, seeing the budget line pivot in or out, and where the new budget line cuts the highest indifference curve gives another point on a demand curve.

## *Income and Substitution Effects (Hicks Method)*

When prices rise consumer demand will naturally change too, with the response in consumption comprising both an 'income effect' adjustment to the change in real income as individuals can no longer afford a good, and also a 'substitution effect' adjustment to the change in relative prices as they turn to better value alternatives. This idea was outlined earlier and the following diagram shows the process using what is known as the 'Hicks' method, with income and substitution effects both visible separately for a normal good where more of the good is preferred to less. The diagram looks complicated but it simply combines factors that have already been explained.

# Income and substitution effects

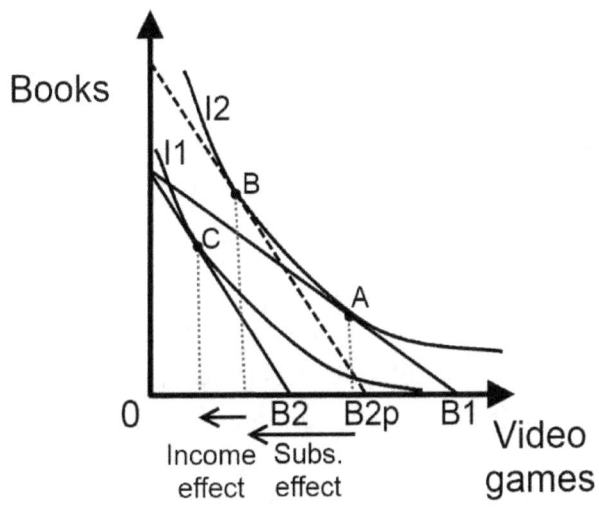

The line labelled B1 is the original budget constraint line showing the maximum possible consumption opportunities given a consumer's income level and the prices of goods, and A is the original point an individual will pick as they perform constrained utility maximization to target the highest available indifference curve, I2. In this example video games rise in price to see the budget line pivot inwards on the x-axis from B1 to B2 where fewer video games can be afforded, but the point on the y-axis remains the same as before as book prices are unaffected.

A substitution effect shows how a change in relative prices affects consumer preferences, and to represent this in diagram form the dashed budget line B2p is drawn parallel from new budget line B2, until the slope and new relative prices are tangent to the previously available utility level (indifference curve I2) at point B. With the new budget line and relative prices it's now point B that a consumer would select on indifference curve I2, and the difference between A and B is the substitution effect.

But budget line B2 is the real constraint that a consumer now has to face, and where this line is tangent to the highest available indifference curve, point C on I1, is the new equilibrium point of constrained utility maximization. The difference between point B where a consumer finds himself after the substitution effect and the final outcome point C gives the income effect.

While the substitution effect will always be negative for a price rise and positive for a price fall, the income effect won't follow the same pattern with non-normal goods. Inferior goods will see the income effect go in the opposite direction due to different indifference curves, and with Giffen goods this opposite direction income effect even dominates the substitution effect and a price rise will see increased consumption of a good.

### *Income and Substitution Effects (Slutsky Method)*

The previous analysis has used diagram gave the Hicks method to find income and substitution effects, but there's also a 'Slutsky' method that uses a slightly different approach. With the Slutsky method the parallel budget line B2p is not set at a point where it's tangent to the indifference curve of the original equilibrium, but is drawn right through the original equilibrium point A. This sees a larger substitution effect and a smaller income effect than the Hicks method.

## *Revealed Preference Theory*

Instead of using indifference curves and preferences to see how price changes will alter consumption patterns, it's possible to use consumer behaviour when faced with price changes to find income and substitution effects or indifference curves. Samuelson's revealed preference theory examines the choice of consumption pattern with one set of prices, before changing a price for a new budget line to reveal a different preferred choice, with a line drawn parallel from the new budget constraint through the original consumption (Slutsky method) to separate the consumption change into substitution and income effects. The following diagram gives the idea.

Line B1 gives the original budget constraint and real world behaviour may reveal point A to be a consumer's chosen consumption pattern, before an increase in the price of video games creates the new budget constraint B2 where point C is now the preferred choice. The parallel line B2p is drawn through original choice of point A, and with this same set of (new) relative prices but adjusted income to allow the potential to select the original choice of point A, a consumer actually selects a different point, B.

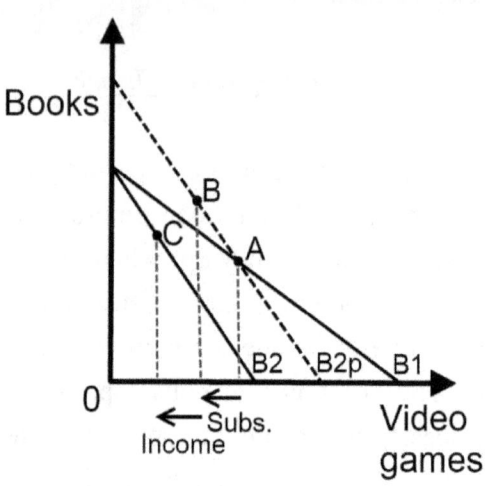

The change in quantity of video games between point A and B is the substitution effect, and from B to C is the income effect. As shown earlier A and B lie on the same indifference curve, and therefore revealed preference can be used to create a preference set for an individual.

# 6 Firm Supply and Costs

*Inputs and Outputs*

After examining consumers and the demand side of the market the next step is to look at producers and the supply side in greater depth. Producers supply the market through the process of production, where resource inputs with limited market value are used to create a different resource output which are valued more highly by the market.

$$INPUT \longrightarrow THE\ FIRM \longrightarrow OUTPUT$$

There are three basic input types or factors of production that a firm can use to produce any range of output for the market; land, human labour, and capital. Land is self-explanatory, labour may refer to the work an individual does themselves or that others do on their behalf, and capital includes everything from financial assets to infrastructure to tools, machines and factories.

While labour is a variable factor of production that can be changed with ease, either by the firm owner working additional hours directly or by hiring new workers, land is a more fixed factor of production that is not so easily adjusted. Capital falls somewhere between the other two factors, and while financial assets, infrastructure or factories can reliably be changed in the long-run it may be difficult to adjust this factor in the short-run. This is because capital factors are more expensive than labour and it will take time to generate the required funds, while it also takes time to build buildings or to produce machinery.

## *The Law of Variable Proportions*

At the start of this book the production possibilities frontier explained the diminishing returns to production based around the idea of limited productive opportunities, and this problem stems from the different flexibility of the three factors of production; land, labour and capital. One of the most fundamental laws of economics is the law of variable proportions, which states that increasing one factor while holding others constant will eventually see diminishing returns for the increased factor, as the proportions are moved out of alignment. Relating this back to labour, capital and land, in the short-run where only variable factors of production (labour) can be altered a move to increase this one factor may initially and temporarily increase output, but with fixed and variable factors moved out of proportion this strategy will soon result in diminishing returns. In simple terms hiring more workers will only be effective so long as you have spare capital (machines, buildings) and land for them.

Moving labour and capital/land out of alignment will first affect marginal and then average returns, as diminishing returns become negative returns and the firm suffers a loss. But with capital and land fixed in the short-run a firm can't avoid these diminishing returns.

*Diminishing Returns to Short-Run Production*

Diminishing returns to production in the short-run (SR) are shown in the following diagram to explain the concept in greater detail, and the marginal physical product (MPP) represents the gain in output made from employing one additional worker. As first this shows increasing returns with the output growing steadily until point Q1, after which the output from each additional worker starts to decline for diminishing returns.

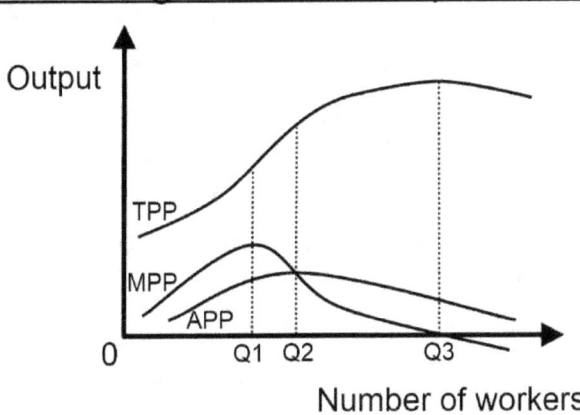

The total physical product (TPP) gives a cumulative total of the MPP, and this follows the marginal curve with diminishing returns from point Q1 on. Dividing the value of the TPP by the number of workers gives the average physical product (APP) for each worker, and at point Q2 where the MPP cuts it from above both marginal and average curves have diminishing but positive returns. This continues until point Q3 where the number of workers is so high that they offer nothing but problems, as the marginal return (MPP) becomes negative to cause the total physical product to fall for the first time. Q3 workers therefore gives the maximum possible output for the firm.

## *A Firm's Choice of SR Production Level*

From a firm's point of view this diagram separates short-run production into three key stages. First there's the stage of increasing returns between the point with zero workers and a Q2 number of workers, and in this range the average physical product (APP) is increasing. The second stage is that of diminishing returns between a Q2 and Q3 level of workers, and over this range the MPP and APP curves are all decreasing but positive. Finally the third stage is that of negative returns beyond point Q3, as the marginal physical product keeps on decreasing to become negative, and the firm begins to see a loss in output as total physical product falls from its maximum.

Every firm wants to operate in the second stage with diminishing returns and specifically right at the end of the second stage at point Q3, as before this point there are still further output gains to be had and the TPP is not yet at its maximum, but after Q3 the TPP will do nothing but fall and therefore more workers should be avoided.

## *Short-Run Costs*

With a firm's short-run production and output it's possible to find their short-run costs. Short-run costs are naturally separated into the same categories as production; fixed or variable, and total, average or marginal costs:

Total cost = total fixed cost + total variable cost (TC = TFC + TVC);

Average fixed cost = total fixed cost divided by quantity of output (AFC = TFC / Q);

Average variable cost = total variable cost divided by output (AVC = TVC / Q);

Marginal cost = the change in total cost caused by a change in one unit of output (MC = $\Delta$AVC / $\Delta$TPP);

Average total cost = total cost divided by output (ATC = TC / Q = AFC + AVC).

At the start of this book it was explained that diminishing returns are linked with a rising opportunity cost, and if diminishing returns give increasing costs it follows that with increasing returns a firm will see decreasing costs. The previous diagram showed that short-run production (marginal, average and total) begins with increasing returns to production before diminishing returns set in, and short-run (SR) costs therefore begin with decreasing costs before this becomes increasing costs.

## Total SR costs for a producing firm

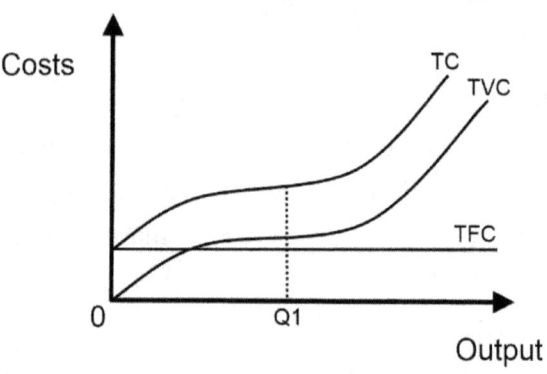

Total fixed costs (TFC) are constant as they're fixed, but total costs (TC) show a decreasing trend at first before diminishing returns to production set in at point Q1 and costs increase. Total variable costs (TVC) are simply the difference between TC and TFC.

Average and marginal costs follow the same trend as total costs with decreasing curves for lower output before the trend turns to increasing costs, with the only exception being average fixed costs (AFC) that decline consistently as output rises because AFC averages out the straight line TFC over ever increasing output.

## Average and marginal SR firm costs

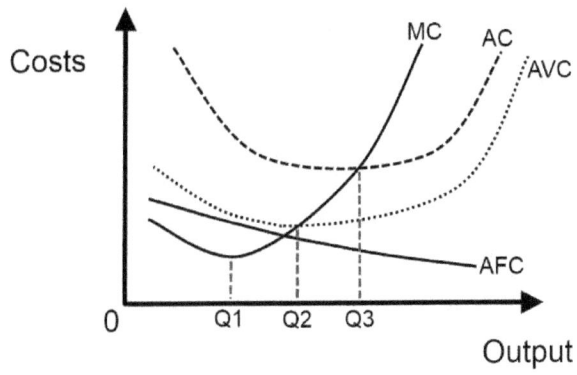

At Q1 diminishing returns set in for marginal costs (MC), at Q2 this happens to average variable costs (AVC) too as the MC curve cuts it from below, and at Q3 where MC cuts the average cost (AC) curve from below all non-fixed costs see diminishing returns. A firm will want to avoid setting production levels below Q3 as the marginal cost of additional output there is below average, and low cost production opportunities are still available.

### *Long-Run Costs*

While the short-run average cost curve (SRAC) is U-shaped as the previous diagram shows, the long-run average cost (LRAC) curve has a flatter dish-shaped curve as it originates from many different SRAC curves, and the points on a LRAC represent a tangent to a SRAC curve.

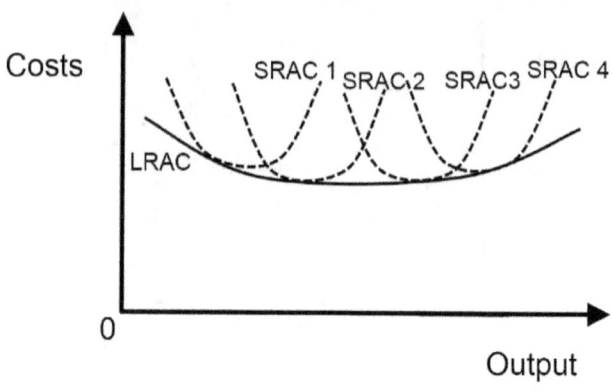

A LRAC curve has lower costs than the SRAC curves as the diagram shows, but there are still visible diminishing returns to production as the long-run curve increases in steepness halfway along its width. This is the starting point for long-run costs as they're based around the summation of multiple sets of short-run costs, but this need not remain the case. In the long-run all factors of production can be altered and there are no fixed costs unlike in the short-run, and therefore the diminishing returns explained by the law of variable proportions are not inevitable. With all factors of production variable the LRAC cost curve is essentially a planning curve that a firm uses as a guide to adjust production and lower costs, made possible by the increased opportunities available in the long-run.

## *Economies of Scale and Economies of Scope*

When all factors of production are variable in the long-run a firm can adjust capital as well as labour, which allows for possible of economies of scale or scope to push down costs. Economies of scale are achieved when greater production reduces the cost of further output, and this may be based around reaching a minimum efficient technical size which reduces wasted resources. Economies of scope are achieved when there are cost reductions by combining production areas, and this may occur if a production division has spare capacity that another could put to use, when there are cost complementarities, or if inputs acquired by one can be used by others at no extra cost.

Economies of scale or scope can lower LR marginal costs (LRMC), and average costs (LRAC) will follow:

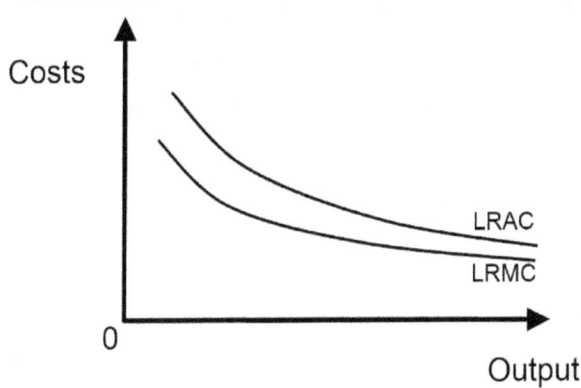

## *Diseconomies of Scale*

Just as a firm may use their ability to adjust all factors of production in the long-run to create economies of scale or scope the opposite can also happen, and a firm may lose control of variable factors and cause diseconomies of scale. This would see the opposite outcome to the diagram above, as the LRMC curve would be on an upward trend as output rises and the LRAC curve would follow it, and this could be caused by any number of inefficiencies linked with greater production. A larger firm may have multiple managers who cause discord as they compete for influence, and the same could also happen at lower levels.

## *External Economies or Diseconomies of Scale*

There are also external economies or diseconomies of scale caused by variables outside of a firm's control. Technological advances in society can lower costs and improve productivity for external economies of scale, but an economic downturn which reduces productivity on a national scale could cause external diseconomies, with a national worker strike that affects the labour supply an example of this occurring on a temporary basis. A longer-run example of external diseconomies of scale may be a declining education system which makes productive workers harder to find.

# 7 Factors of Production

*Substitutability of Production Factors*

External factors beyond a firm's control can have a big impact on its output and costs and can potentially limit the availability of factors of production, even in the long-run. But if a firm could substitute labour (L) for capital (K) without losing output, and vice versa, then it may be able to manage any external shocks and prevent productivity losses.

The worst case for a firm is zero substitutability between factors, and with both labour and capital needed to raise output (X) a shock to one could be devastating. This is known as fixed proportions Leontief technology, and is shown in the following diagram with the dashed line the only possible combination of the capital (K) and labour (L) factors of production.

Output (X) is a function (F) of the level of capital (K) and labour (L), $X = F(K, L)$, and with zero substitutability between factors they are perfect complements and a minimum level of each production factor will be required to raise the level of output:

Leontief fixed proportions: $X = \min(K, L)$

## Fixed proportions Leontief technology

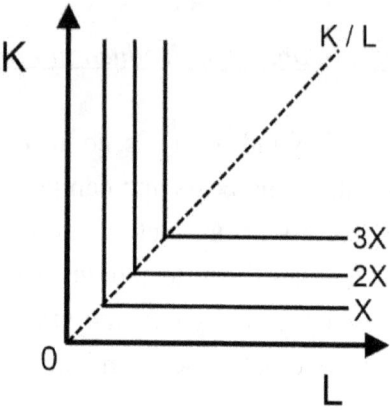

The best case scenario for a firm would be for there to be perfect substitutability between capital and labour factors of production, and this would allow limitless possible combinations of the two factors with no loss in the firm's output. Output would simply be the summation of capital and labour factors, where 'a' and 'b' in the formula below represent the level of capital and labour respectively:

Perfect substitutability: $X = aK + bL$

Perfect substitutability is shown in the following diagram.

## Perfect substitutability

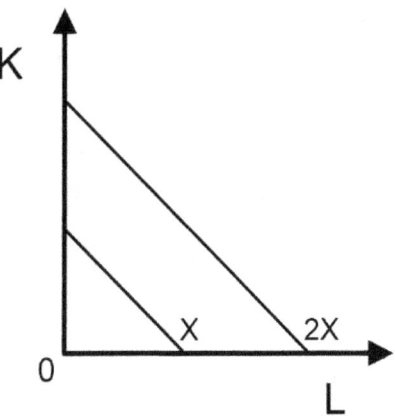

## *Cobb-Douglas Production Functions*

In practice most production functions are thought to behave somewhere between these two extremes, with variable proportions possible yet imperfect substitutability ensuring that the factors will affect each other. This is known as a Cobb-Douglas production function and is shown in the following diagram, with the output (X) determined by the function:

$$X = aK^bL^c$$

The power/exponent variables, b and c, determine the returns to scale and the relationship between inputs and output:

$b + c > 1$ gives increasing returns to scale
$b + c = 1$ gives constant returns to scale
$b + c < 1$ gives decreasing returns to scale

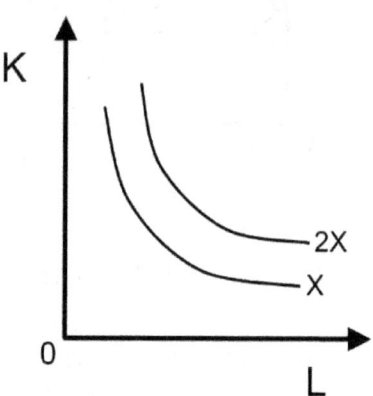

## Cobb-Douglas production function

*Returns to Scale*

With increasing returns to scale the output grows at a faster rate than inputs (e.g. 2 x inputs gives more than 2 x output), with constant returns to scale output grows at the same rate as inputs (e.g. 2 x inputs equals 2 x output), and decreasing returns to scale sees output grow at a slower rate than inputs (e.g. 2 x inputs gives less than 2 x output).

The returns to scale gives the effects of all factors of production together while returns looks at one factor, and it's therefore possible for the two to show different trends.

## Constant returns to scale and diminishing returns

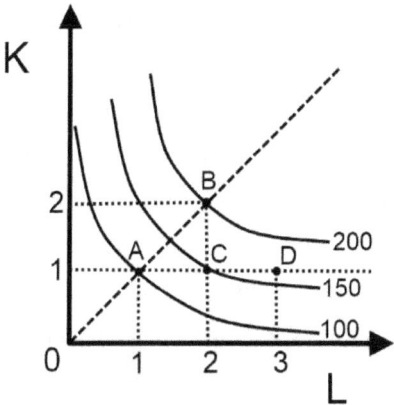

In this diagram there are both constant returns to scale and diminishing returns. With both capital (K) and labour (L) factors combined production shows constant returns to scale, as 1K + 1L = 100 output at point A, while 2K + 2L = 200 output at point B. But labour shows diminishing returns if examined on its own, and with capital held constant at one. From point A to point C labour is raised by one unit from 1 to 2 and output increases from 100 to 150, a multiple of 1.5 and output gain of 50. But between point C and D labour is again raised by one unit from 2 to 3, but the output gain is below the curve giving output of 200, showing an output gain below 50 and a multiple gain far below 1.5 for diminishing returns.

## *Producer Theory Similarity to Consumer Theory*

Cobb-Douglas, perfect substitutability, and Leontief fixed proportions diagrams may seem familiar, and that's because they're the same diagrams that were seen earlier for consumer demand. With consumers the curves represented their indifference and preferences, the foundation of demand, and here the curves represent firm production possibilities, the foundation of supply. This knowledge makes the analysis easier and much of what has already been learned can be applied to production.

## *Isoquant Curves*

Firm or producer theory uses isoquant curves (in place of consumer theory's indifference curves) and each curve represents the different minimum quantities of inputs needed to create a given level of output or TPP (in place of consumer theory's utility), and as more is naturally preferred to less a firm prefers a higher curve to a lower one. Any point on the isoquant curve gives a different marginal rate of technical substitution (MRTS):

$$MRTS_{(K\ to\ L)} = - \Delta K / \Delta L = MPP_L / MPP_K$$

$MRTS_{(K\ to\ L)}$ falls with a move down the isoquant due to diminishing marginal rate of factor substitution, and the opposite MRTS$_{(L \text{ to } K)}$ will rise further down the curve and can be found by reversing the L and K values in the above formula.

## *Isocost Lines*

Production limits are defined by an isocost line, which is similar to a consumer's budget constraint line but utility maximization is replaced by cost minimization. An isocost line shows the different combinations of inputs with the same total cost given relative production factor prices. The isocost equation depends upon the rental rate of capital r, the amount of capital used K, the wage rate of labour w, and the level of labour employed L, and shows the total cost C for capital and labour, while the slope of the isocost line weights the cost of capital against the cost of labour as follows:

$$\text{Isocost equation: } rK + wL = C$$
$$\text{Slope} = -w/r$$

## *Equilibrium in Production*

A production equilibrium is reached where the marginal rate of transformation, MRTS, of the isoquant curve is tangent to the lowest isocost line. This situation is represented in the following equation and diagram:

$$MRTS_{(K \text{ to } L)} = - w/r$$

## Isoquant and isocost equilibrium point

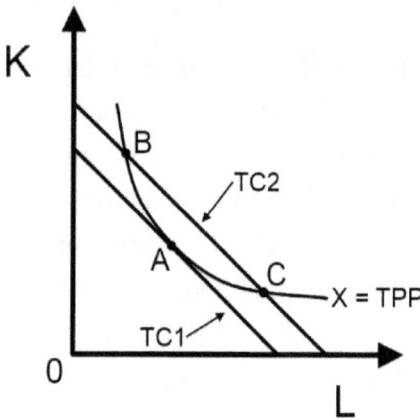

Point A is the equilibrium point here, where the isoquant curve with output of X or TPP (total physical product) is tangent to the isocost line TC1 (total costs 1). Point B and C also see the isoquant and isocost lines meet, but the firm will select point A instead as these alternative points require more inputs and give a higher total cost on isocost line TC2, yet don't offer a higher output in return (= X).

But the efficient equilibrium result may only be possible in the long-run and in the short-run the capital factor of production may not be variable, which could see capital fixed at a level below point A. This would leave an inferior point such as C, with the same output but higher costs, as the best available production option for a firm.

If the prices of either capital (K) or labour (L) changed then the isocost line would change accordingly. A rise in the wage rate of labour (w) or the rental rate of capital (r) would see the isocost line pivot inwards on the relevant axis respectively, putting the producer on a different isoquant curve. This is similar to the way that changes in prices push a consumer onto a different indifference curve, and it's possible to isolate the separate effects of this change in cost in the same way except that instead of income and substitution effects, isoquant and isocost analysis gives output and substitution effects.

# 8 Market Power and Profit Maximization

### *Firm Profit*

A firm is concerned first and foremost with the maximization of its level of profits, and therefore the primary motivator of the firm's level of supply will be the level of output which offers the highest profit. Profit is defined in two ways in economics, either as normal profit or economic profit (also known as abnormal or supernormal profit). Normal profit is the return that reflects only the risk a firm takes on with their investment, and is just enough to keep a firm from exiting that activity. It sees a firm cut even as total revenue (TR) - total costs (TC) equals zero. Economic or abnormal profit represents an excess over normal profit and arises from market power, where a firm can set a price and output level that sees TR - TC exceed zero.

### *Lerner Index for Measuring Market Power*

While every firm may like to set prices high and earn abnormal profit many lack the power to do so. The Lerner index (L) shows a firm's market power, measured by the ability to set price (P) above marginal cost (MC), due to a low own price elasticity of demand (PED):

$$L = (P - MC) / P = -1 / PED$$

L is between 0 and 1 and high values suggest greater market power. In a competitive industry L is low as firms face substitute products for a high PED, and prices are held at marginal cost as firms are price takers who can't decide their prices. In an uncompetitive industry L is high and firms are price makers which can choose their prices.

*Profit for Price-Taking Firms*

If firms are price takers then this diagram will apply:

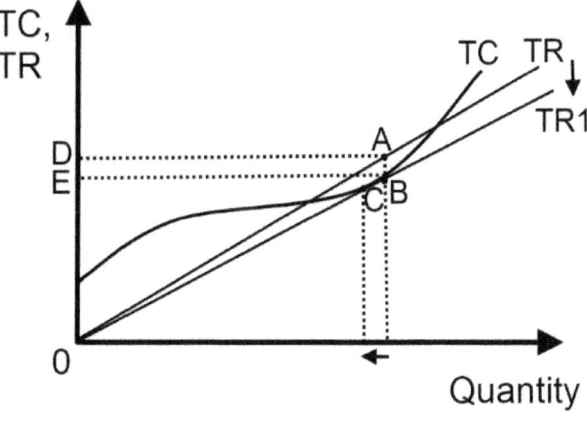

A firm may begin at point A on the total revenue curve (TR) based on a high price (P) and high quantity of output (Q), where TR = P x Q. At this point total revenue exceeds total costs (TC) by the largest amount, for an economic profit given by the difference between points D and E. But this abnormal profit attracts new firms into the industry, and the increased competition sees the market price forced down to marginal cost as firms try to undercut each other to win sales. All firms are now price takers, and any attempt to raise prices will see consumers abandon them for lower priced competitors. With a now reduced market price the TR curve will shift down to TR1 (as TR1 = P x Q), and total revenue will be lower at every quantity of output level.

If a firm stays with the same level of output that took it to the lucrative point A then it will operate at point B, and the firm will face a loss as at point B total revenue (now TR1) is below total costs (TC). To escape this situation the firm will reduce the quantity of its output to move along its total revenue line from B to point C, where TR = TC. While this doesn't offer abnormal profits it does give normal profit that covers costs and risk, and as the diagram suggests this is the best the price-taking firm can do as every other point on the TR1 line is below the TC curve.

## *Profit for Price-Making Firms*

The scenario facing a firm with market power which can set its own prices differs from that of a price-taking firm. For simplicity assumptions include a linear demand curve (i.e. straight line downward sloping), constant marginal (and therefore average) costs, and no fixed costs. This would make MC = AC and both costs would be represented with the same horizontal line, and this situation suggests a firm has perfectly elastic supply. Total costs (TC) would therefore also be a straight line, but upward sloping with quantity as TC = AC x Q.

Average revenue (AR) is given by the demand curve, as it represents the market price for a given quantity. Total revenue (TR) = P x Q, and therefore total revenue will start at zero where Q = 0 and end at zero as P = 0, rising and then falling between the two points. This is drawn as a semi-circle shape, with the assumption that price and quantity can be divided into infinitesimally small numbers.

The other factor required to show profit maximization for a firm with market power is marginal revenue (MR). The marginal revenue gives the change (derivative) in total revenue and can be found with differentiation of the total revenue function, and the total revenue function in turn can be found using a demand function.

A linear demand function (D = AR) has the following form, where P is price, Q is quantity, 'a' is the intercept on the y-axis and 'b' the slope of the demand curve:

$$P = a - bQ$$

Total revenue, TR, equals P or AR multiplied by Q:

$$TR = aQ - bQ^2$$

Differentiation multiplies the coefficient variable (i.e. a and b here) by the power, then reduces the power by one:

$$MR = a - 2bQ$$

A slope of -2bQ is twice as steep as the linear demand curve's slope of -bQ, to give MR its form.

The following diagram combines all of the analysis.

The top diagram gives total revenue (TR) and total costs (TC), while the lower one examines marginal and average revenue (MR, AR) and costs (MC, AC). It may seem likely that profit maximization would occur with a Q2 level of output, as this is where total revenue is highest and MR = 0, meaning all available revenue has been claimed and there's no more to gain, and this was how optimal output was decided earlier. But on inspection this point is unsuitable as MR is below MC, and a firm will earn nothing but still face additional marginal costs.

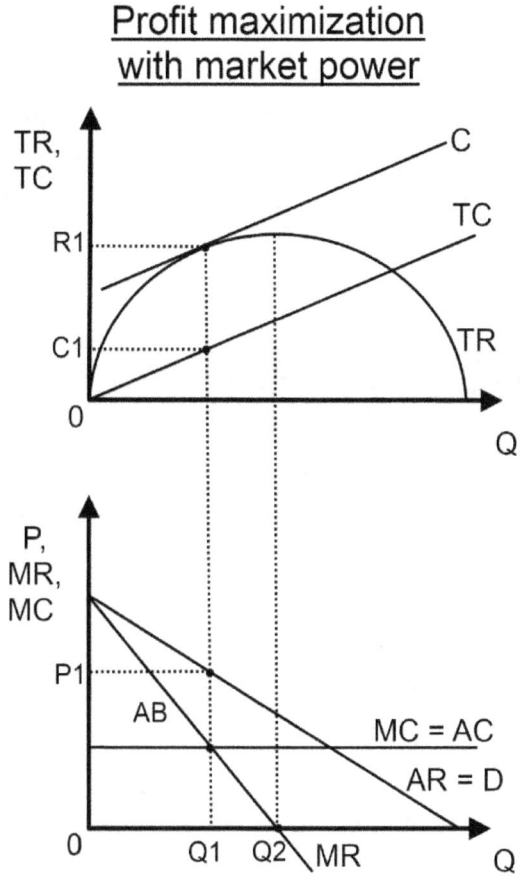

Profit maximization occurs at output quantity Q1 and at this point TR exceeds TC by the largest amount, while the declining MR equals MC and there are no further gains to be had (where MR > MC), and any further output will incur a loss (where MR < MC). The tangent to the total revenue TR curve, C, is parallel to the TC cost curve at quantity Q1, and this identical slope signals that the change in revenue equals the change in costs, confirming that MR = MC here. Selecting this output quantity Q1 for price P1 on the demand curve earns the firm with market power the abnormal profit given by the rectangle AB.

## *Principal Agent Problem*

However, although market power may allow a firm to generate superior profits this may not necessarily come to pass. The manager acting on a firm's behalf may use its market power for his own gain and not to maximize profit for the firm's stakeholders (employees, shareholders, suppliers, the wider community, and government). This is known as the principal-agent problem, and to ensure a manager does their job properly contractual incentives will usually be required to align the interests of the principal (firm) and the agent (manager) acting on its behalf. Performance related contracts are designed to ensure the agent has the incentive to exert effort which comes at a personal cost, and the central focus is to make the manager a participant in firm activity so that his goals match those of the firm.

# 9 Perfect and Monopolistic Competition

*Market Structure and Market Power*

A firm's market power depends upon the market structure, and a more favourable structure will give a firm greater power and greater opportunity to reach its goals. The following diagram shows the relationship between the two.

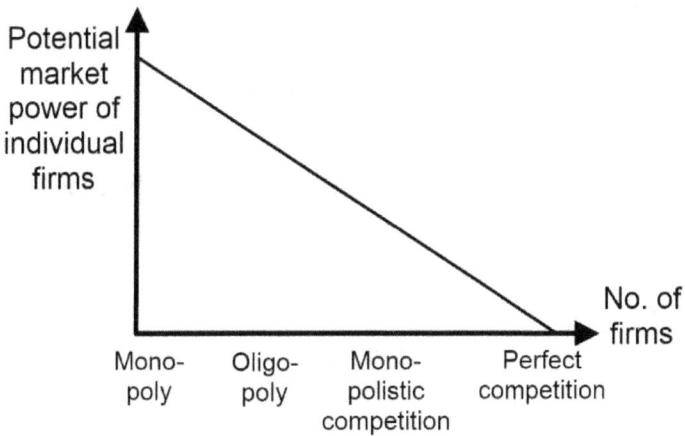

This section examines the two scenarios where a firm will have the least market power; in industries and market structures with monopolistic competition or perfect competition. The lower the level of firm market power the more competition there will be between firms, where competition is defined as sellers of similar products using price and non-price mechanisms to try and attract the largest number of customers. Competition is usually considered good for society as it keeps prices low and supply high.

## *Perfect Competition Defined*

Perfect competition is the benchmark for consumer welfare and may offer allocative efficiency, as demand equals supply and price equals marginal cost and no distribution of income could make one person better off without making another worse off. It also gives productive efficiency, with technical and cost efficiency as inputs are used optimally to generate output, and dynamic efficiency, with SR and LR needs balanced as distributional and productive efficiency support economic growth. These features give a Pareto optimal or best collective outcome.

Features of perfectly competitive markets include many buyers and sellers for small market shares and no market power, no product differentiation for homogenous products and consumer preferences, fully informed buyers and sellers, no transaction costs, no entry or exit barriers, and firms are price takers with no power to affect prices.

## *Perfect Competition Equilibrium*

As all market participants in a perfectly competitive industry are price takers a firm's price is fixed at the equilibrium where market demand meets supply, and this gives horizontal demand (D), average revenue (AR = D) and marginal revenue curves (MR slope is half AR = D, and half of a zero slope is zero again). Familiar cost curves are added to this to complete the following diagram.

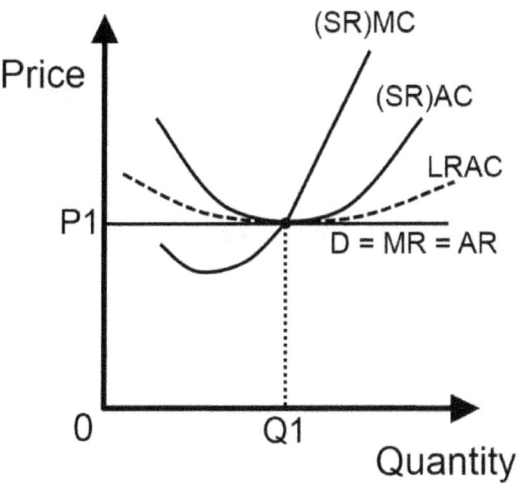

## SR and LR equilibrium under perfect competition

Firm supply in the short-run (SR) is given by the rising part of the marginal cost (SRMC) curve, where

SRMC is over and above short-run variable costs to cover ongoing running costs. The short-run equilibrium occurs where demand (D = AR) equals supply (rising part of SRMC) at P1, Q1, which also sees marginal revenue (MR) equal marginal cost (MC) as firms earn normal profits, or in simple terms firms earn enough to cut even and cover costs but no more than that.

Although the equilibrium and default under perfect competition sees neither abnormal profit nor loss, firms may still face either of these outcomes temporarily due to the steep SR supply (SRMC) curve. If market demand were to rise the demand curve (D = AR = MR) will shift up to raise the equilibrium price and output quantity where MR = MC, and put revenue above average costs to create temporary abnormal profits. But these profits should attract new firms to the industry to shift supply up and restore the equilibrium in the diagram.

If market demand falls the D curve shifts down for a lower equilibrium price and quantity where it equals supply, putting a firm's revenue below its average costs for temporary abnormal losses. This may force a firm out of the industry if MC is below short-run average variable costs, but fewer firms in the industry will reduce supply and should shift the supply curve down to restore the original equilibrium. However, shifts in demand are the exception and the expected outcome in the short-run under perfect competition is normal profits.

In the long-run cost curves are flatter as the capital production factor can be adjusted, and they may resemble the form of the LRAC curve in the diagram, be perfectly flat with constant costs, show an incline with diseconomies of scale, or show a decline with economies of scale. Whichever it is the flatter cost curves give flatter supply curves (firms supply at cost under perfect competition), and with flat demand curves the market is more elastic in its response to shifts and shocks to prevent a firm facing the risk of abnormal profits or losses it may in the short-run. In the long-run under perfect competition firms earn normal profit and cover costs but no more than that.

## *Monopolistic Competition Defined*

Monopolistic competition offers firms greater market power than perfect competition (pc), and typical features include many buyers and suppliers but fewer than pc, product differentiation with branding, firms have their own negatively sloped demand curve which is elastic as other producers offer substitutes, and market entry is quite easy. A good example of such an industry might be fast food.

## *Monopolistic Competition Equilibrium*

The following diagram shows the short-run equilibrium under monopolistic competition. The SR equilibrium occurs with production at Q1 where MR equals MC, and corresponding price on the demand curve P1. This gives an abnormal profit above average costs represented by the rectangle Q1 x (P1 - AC1).

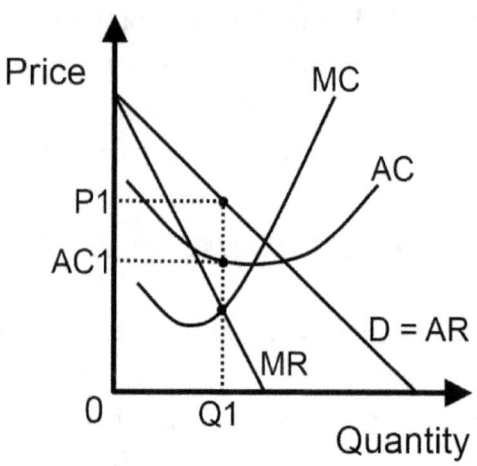

## SR equilibrium under monopolistic competition

But in the long-run the abnormal profits and relatively easy entry in monopolistically competitive markets will attract new entrants into the industry, and they will take demand away from incumbent firms. This will reduce the level of individual demand for all firms and shift the demand curve left, causing the marginal revenue curve that has half the slope of a linear demand curve to also shift left. The results are shown in the next diagram.

The leftward shift of D = AR and MR curves sees them cut the MC and AC curves at a different position in the long-run, and the equilibrium point where MR = MC is now Q2. The corresponding price is P2 and this now equals long-run average costs, as in the long-run industry competition takes away abnormal profits to leave only normal profit where average revenue equals average costs.

## LR equilibrium under monopolisitic competition

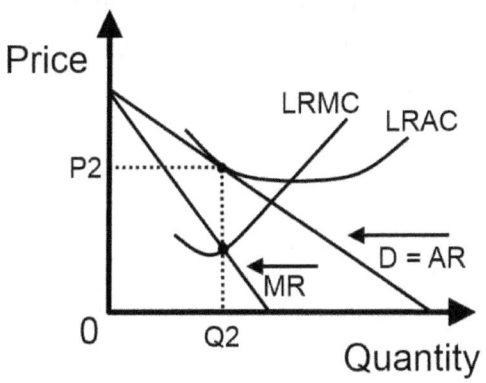

In the short-run a firm in a monopolistically competitive market can count on earning abnormal profits, using their temporary market power to select an output quantity and price that takes advantage of the short-run high demand for their product. But those firms in a perfectly competitive industry have no such market power and should earn only normal profits, although they're powerless to broader market trends and could face shifts in market demand for temporary abnormal profit or losses.

In the long-run competitors take away most of the demand for a firm's products in a monopolistically competitive market to allow only normal profit, while in the long-run in a perfectly competitive market a firm can adjust to any demand shocks that gave unpredictable returns to guarantee a normal profit. Monopolistic and perfectly competitive markets are not identical in the long-run however, and a firm in the former market finds itself further left on its LRAC curve, as the monopolistically competitive firm has a higher equilibrium price and lower equilibrium quantity than its perfectly competitive counterpart, due to different demand curves.

# 10 Monopoly

## *Monopoly Defined*

A monopoly sees a firm have greater market power than any other type of industry structure. This market structure has many buyers but only one seller firm, it involves unique products that can't be easily substituted, and market entry is blockaded to prevent other firms from becoming competitors and challenging the dominant firm. These features allow a monopoly firm to act as a price maker or quantity setter without resistance, and this may have harmful effects for consumers and society at large.

A small market size may facilitate a monopoly structure but monopolies can arise in any number of ways. Sources include political preference, a public sector contract award to a firm (e.g. education provision), cultural reasons (e.g. Halal butcher or Kosher foods), through patents or copyrights and trademarks to protect intellectual property rights, or alternatively because an industry is simply more efficient with only one producer.

## *Monopoly Welfare Effects*

The following diagram shows the potential welfare gains and losses linked with a monopoly, where Pm and

Qm represent the price and quantity of a monopolist, and Ppc and Qpc give a comparison with the perfectly competitive market levels. The MC = AC curve here is horizontal as a monopolist's supply is perfectly elastic.

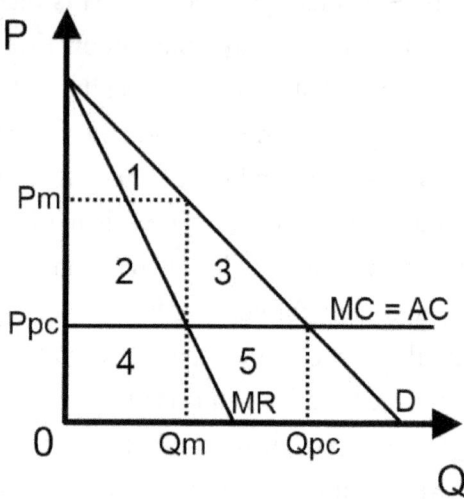

Earlier on in the book the idea of consumer surplus and producer surplus was put forward. The former is the difference between what a consumer would be willing to pay on their demand curve and the market price, while the producer surplus is the difference between what a seller would be willing to pay on their supply curve and the actual market price. If the perfect competition price (Ppc) and quantity (Qpc) gave the equilibrium then areas 1, 2 and 3 (i.e. everything above the cost curves but below the demand curve) would be a consumer surplus, as rectangles 4 and 5 give the cost of resources. But with a monopoly prices and quantity the results are quite different.

In a monopoly the area labelled 4 is the resource cost, while rectangle 5 gives the resources allocated elsewhere because of the lower output quantity. With a monopolist the consumer surplus is only area 1, between Pm and the demand curve, while square 2 shows an abnormal profit caused by market power rather than production efficiency and is the producer surplus here. It represents a transfer of income from consumers to the producer under a monopoly relative to the perfect competition model. Area 3 is Harberger's triangle or the deadweight loss caused by the higher prices and lower quantity of supplied goods from a monopolist, an allocative efficiency loss. The specific sizes of the five areas will vary depending on the elasticity of demand and the steepness of the demand curve.

Overall areas 1 and 4 are identical with both the monopoly and perfect competition equilibrium, while area 5 is only a deployment of firm resources elsewhere due to lower monopoly output, and it has no real impact on society's welfare as the cost of these resources is unchanged. Triangle 3 is the only certain welfare loss and lost consumer surplus, caused by a firm having the market power to ignore society's needs and select its preferred price and supply quantity. Square 2 is a grey area, as income gains are transferred from consumers to producers yet the firm may use this in ways that benefit welfare.

Economist Richard Posner insists that area 2 is a sure welfare loss under monopoly as it represents an abnormal monopoly profit that a firm only achieved through the use of limited resources. In order for a firm to suffer this opportunity cost of used resources, including advertising costs to inform consumers about the product and lobbying or patent costs to secure the monopoly position, the marginal benefits of this investment must be greater than those associated with not chasing the monopoly position. That means that the producer surplus of square 2 must give clear and direct benefits to the firm itself (e.g. higher profits for managers and shareholders), as opposed to shared welfare gains for all (e.g. better value products).

## *Long-Run Monopoly Welfare Effects*

The welfare effects noted apply to the short-run in a monopoly and in the long-run things may be a little different, as efficiency gains are possible due to economies of scale and scope linked with all factors of production being variable in the long-run.

A monopoly may be a good source for innovation in the long-run, as firm profits wouldn't have to be invested in outmanoeuvring rivals and income could be directed to research and development instead. Successful innovation could allow lower long-run average and marginal costs under monopoly as shown in the following diagram, with (LAC = LMC (m)) compared to those under perfect competition (LAC = LMC (pc)). In this case the monopolist's pricing and output levels create only a small deadweight loss of triangle 2, while the firm saves on resource costs and gains the value of rectangle 1. If some of these price savings were passed on to consumers then society may see a net gain from the monopoly.

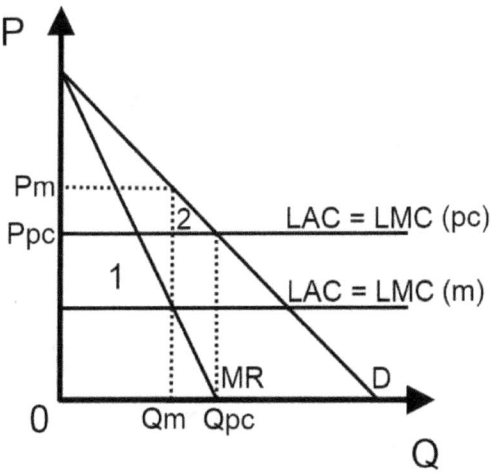

## Monopoly and efficiency

Alternatively, a monopoly can raise inefficiency as without competition to push firms to stay ahead of each other a firm can stagnate and become inefficient in the long-run, resulting in a productivity fall. A less efficient firm can suffer higher long-run average and marginal costs that a counterpart under perfect competition, with LAC = LMC for a monopoly (m) greater than for perfect competition (pc), and this causes welfare losses that exceed those normally associated with a monopoly.

The deadweight loss and allocative inefficiency is not only the usual triangle labelled 2 above monopoly costs, but also the area right below this where a greater quantity could have been produced at a lower cost under perfect competition. And area 1 is now not a saving in resource costs but another welfare loss as resources cost more.

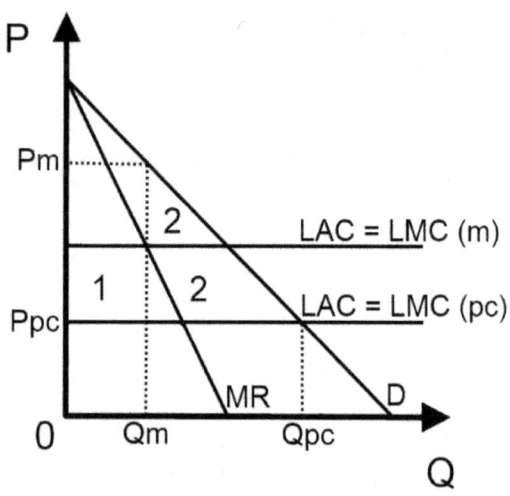

## *Government Intervention to Protect Consumer Welfare*

Government intervention may be required to defend consumers from the welfare losses associated with a monopoly or those with significant market power. State strategies can include price controls to set prices equal to marginal cost, or average cost if this would cause a loss, and a lump sum tax to the value of the abnormal profit which raises average cost but doesn't change the price or output quantity. Another option is a unit tax which shifts the marginal and average cost curves upwards, although this could see the monopolist producer offload some of the cost onto consumers by raising the price or reducing the quantity of supply.

## *Price Discrimination*

If government doesn't step in with regulation then the firm may deviate from a single monopoly price, preferring to use price discrimination to set prices to get the most from each consumer. First degree price discrimination sees a firm with market power set a different price for each consumer based on where they sit on the demand curve, in an attempt to turn the consumer surplus into a profit. But this requires that the firm knows each consumer's willingness to pay, and while better for society than a pure single price monopoly that rips everyone off this multiple price strategy can create distribution issues.

Second degree price discrimination charges customers based on usage rates, with bulk discounts and buy one get one half price promotions some examples of this strategy. While this is again better for society than a monopoly price that ignores consumer needs this also creates distribution issues, as a firm can't know how unit costs will compare to unit profits to plan supply accordingly.

Finally, there is third degree price discrimination where different prices are charged to various types of consumer, such as in different countries, in education or professional sectors, and commercial clients relative to domestic ones. A monopolist will exploit differences in elasticity between markets, and a low elasticity market will be charged a higher price, while those in more elastic markets are charged less. This shares both the benefits and issues linked with price discrimination in general.

# 11 Oligopoly

## *Oligopoly Defined*

The last type of market structure to be examined is oligopoly, where there are many buyers and few sellers with large market shares. With two firms this is known as a duopoly but there can be several firms in an oligopoly, and their market shares may be asymmetric with some dominant players and others on the fringe. Sellers in oligopoly often sell differentiated products and compete with non-price methods, and the market structure is known for interdependence where any move from one firm is likely to see a response, while high entry barriers make it difficult for new firms to enter the industry. Examples include the car industry, and package holidays.

## *Kinked Demand Curve*

One feature that may be seen in an oligopoly is a kinked demand curve, where there are essentially two market demand curves that keep market prices at a stable level. In this situation a firm won't lower prices as demand is inelastic below its current price and a price cut won't see greater sales profits, but a firm also can't raise prices as demand is elastic above its current price and a higher price will reduce their sales quantity and profits.

In the following diagram the current market price is at point A and the solid lines represent the kinked market demand line that a firm faces, with hashed lines showing the rest of the separate elastic and inelastic demand curves.

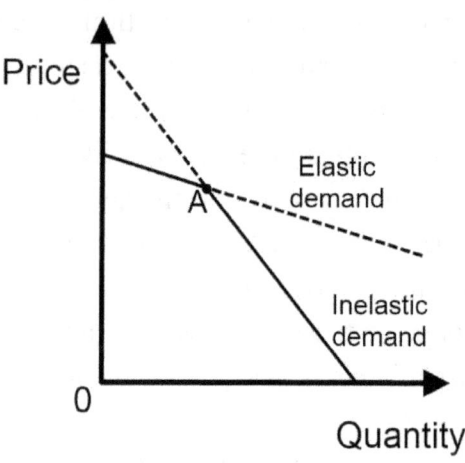

## Kinked demand curve

With two demand curves there are two marginal revenue (MR) curves with slopes half as steep, but this creates an MR curve discontinuity as in the next diagram.

This kinked demand curve and discontinuity in the MR curve creates an opportunity for a firm in an oligopoly, as the equilibrium is decided where marginal revenue and marginal costs (MC) are equal but a firm would have the same price and quantity levels irrespective of whether this occurs at point B or C. This allows a firm to change its cost patterns without any ill effects, for example between MC and MC1, and these cost changes may facilitate better strategies to compete with rivals.

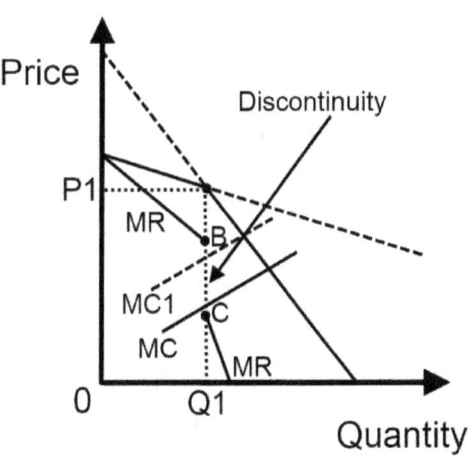

## Discontinuity in MR

*Cartels*

Cartels may be found in oligopoly market structures, defined as any explicit or tacit agreement between firms to control price or market share. The cartel essentially operates as a multi-firm monopolist with a rising marginal cost supply curve, and the cartel equilibrium price (Pcar) is higher and quantity (Qcar) lower than perfect competition.

## Cartel equilibrium

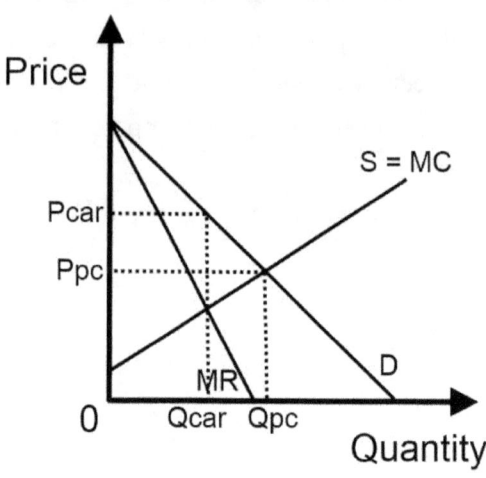

A cartel is more likely to form when a lower number of firms are involved, as it's easier to keep participants in line when there are fewer of them. Similar costs and products that will naturally make firms interests more aligned are another supportive factor, as is a stable economic environment because a cartel depends upon stability in firm behaviour where many firms act as one. Cartels are usually imaged as being horizontal where firms have similar levels of power, such as with oil suppliers, but they may also be vertical as in the case of distributors following supplier trends to withhold resources from certain markets.

## *Dominant Firm Price Leadership*

Another type of oligopoly may contain one large firm which holds a significant market share and takes the majority of total sales, while the rest of the firms in the industry supply the remainder of the market. In this situation the large firm may behave differently to the others and act as a dominant firm, taking the lead to set prices at a level that maximizes their own profits.

The following diagram shows the case of a dominant firm price leadership industry. The demand for a dominant firm's products receive will simply be the remaining market demand after the other firms have supplied their products, and therefore the starting point for a dominant firm's demand (D leader) is the difference between market demand (D market) and the supply of other firms (S other firms). The end point for a dominant firm's demand curve is where it merges with market demand, and this occurs at a point where the supply of other firms is at a zero quantity.

As always with a linear demand curve the marginal revenue for the dominant leading firm (MR leader) is half as steep as the relevant demand curve (D leader), and the point where this cuts the dominant firm's marginal cost curve (MC leader) determines the profit maximizing price on its demand curve. This gives a price for the dominant firm of Pl and output quantity Ql at point L.

## Dominant firm price leadership

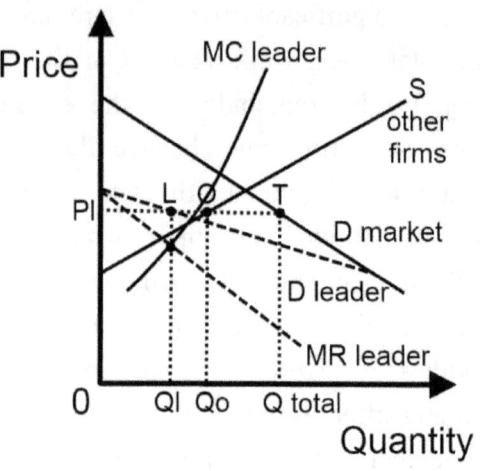

The dominant firm's price leadership sets a price that the other firms follow and it therefore also decides their output level, at quantity Qo at point O on their supply curve, for a total quantity of Q total on the market demand curve at point T.

## Cournot Oligopoly

If the oligopoly is tighter with a greater level of interdependence then firms may not simply react to what other firms are doing, but try to forecast what they will do in advance and act accordingly, a situation known as Cournot oligopoly. In this type of market structure firms don't compete on price but with quantity, and firms are thought to make assumptions that a competitor's output quantity will be fixed at a certain amount and then set their own output at a corresponding profit maximizing level.

In a two firm duopoly situation where one firm is expected to produce no output the other would essentially be a monopolist, and act accordingly to select an output quantity where its marginal revenue equals marginal cost to maximize profit. And if the other firm was expected to produce the output level that matched the entire industry's supply needs, as with perfect competition, then a firm would produce zero output to maximize its profits as abnormal profits aren't available in perfect competition. Joining these two points for a firm gives its reaction curve, and where both of the two duopoly firms' reaction curves cross is where the two reactions will balance, and therefore the Cournot equilibrium expected outcome.

In the following diagram the point where the 'firm 1 reaction curve' touches the Q2 axis represents a point of high Q2 (monopoly output for firm 2), and the reaction of zero Q1 (no output for firm 1). And where the firm 1 reaction curve touches the Q1 axis represents a point of zero Q2 (no output for firm 2), and the reaction of high Q1 (monopoly output for firm 1). The 'firm 2 reaction curve' shows the opposite scenario for firm 2, with the same relationships as just mentioned except with Q1 and Q2, and firm 1 and firm 2, switched.

If one firm in a duopoly had a first mover advantage in quantity choice due to greater knowledge of costs and industry demand then a different 'Stackelberg equilibrium' (St in the diagram) may result. If firm 1 had the first mover advantage then it could select the highest possible quantity Q1 on its reaction curve and commit to it, leaving firm 2 to respond with the corresponding level of Q2 output based on its own reaction curve. The Cournot equilibrium would then be impossible as firm 1 would have already committed to a higher level of output, and the Stackelberg result shown in the diagram would instead occur as an outcome. This would see first mover firm 1 with higher output and profit, and firm 2 with lower output and profit, than under the Cournot equilibrium.

## Cournot equilibrium

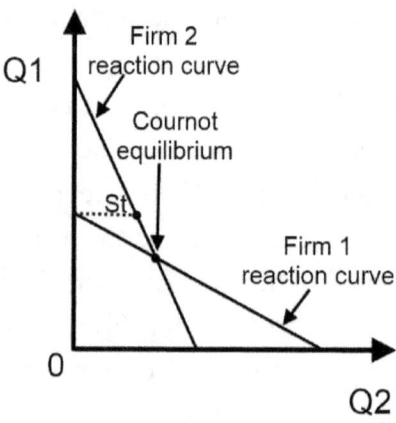

## Equilibrium Comparisons

The two firm Cournot equilibrium sees lower output than under perfect competition, but greater output than a collusive equilibrium where monopoly profits are shared.

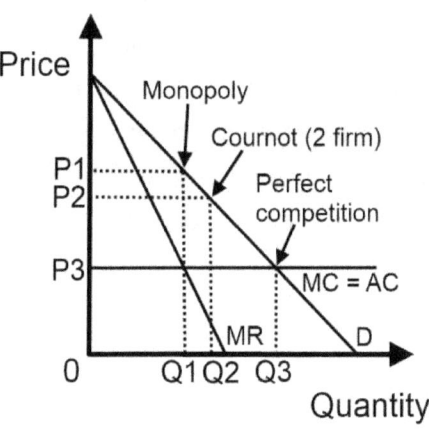

The Cournot equilibrium in the diagram refers to a two firm duopoly and in a Cournot oligopoly with more firms the result would be different. As more firms are added to the analysis the Cournot equilibrium quantity rises and the related equilibrium price will fall, and this sees a move down the demand curve toward the perfectly competitive outcome with a large number of firms.

Cournot competition is based on firms competing on quantity but Bertrand argued that firms in a duopoly will compete on price, as this is considered to be what consumers care most about and therefore a more effective way to compete. Bertrand price competition sees the two duopoly firms constantly lower price as they each have the incentive to undercut the other to gain greater sales, and this gives an equilibrium where price equals marginal cost (P = MC) as in perfect competition. It's only at this point where firms can't afford to follow their incentives and undercut their rival further, and this can be the only long-run equilibrium with price competition, giving the same output quantity and price as in perfect competition. This idea of price being forced down to marginal cost is examined further in the next section.

# 12 Games

The study of Microeconomics has shown interdependence among those involved in the market, as the outcomes facing firms and consumers are affected by the actions of both their peers, and those on the other side of the buyer-seller divide. When decision makers know that their actions affect each other and take this into account before choosing their strategy, as it's in their best interests to do so, then the interaction may be represented as a game. All games have rules, strategies and payoffs, and a player can end up as a winner, a loser, or neither. A model known as game theory is used to represent the specific details and to make predictions for the outcome of the game.

### *Duopoly Game*

The following diagram is a game between two competing firms in a duopoly market structure. Each firm has a choice of two different strategies and can either set a high or low price for their products, but both firms must make their choice of price simultaneously and can't wait to see what their rival does. The outcomes of the game can be found by looking in the box where the two firm's chosen strategies meet, with firm one's payoffs the left of each pair, while firm two's payoffs are the right of each pair.

## A duopoly pricing game

|  | Firm 2 | |
|---|---|---|
|  | High price | Low price |
| **Firm 1** High price | 100, 100 | -10, 150 |
| **Firm 1** Low price | 150, -10 | 0, 0 |

In this game there are four possible outcomes for a firm, and if both firms set a high price they share abnormal profits like a cartel to earn 100 each. But if both compete and set a low price then price falls to the level of marginal cost like a perfectly competitive market, and firms earn normal profit of a 0 (risk-adjusted) return. If one sets a high price as the other goes lower the undercutting firm gains a large sales share for a 150 payoff, as the higher priced firm suffers a net loss of -10 due to lack of sales.

To predict the outcome of the game the payoffs linked with each of the two pricing strategies can be examined further, and firms will decide on the option that offers the higher payoff. If one strategy gives a higher payoff irrespective of the actions of the other firm then it's the dominant strategy for a firm, and this can be found by simply eliminating the opposite and ruling out those dominated strategies that always offer a lower payoff.

If the other firm selects a high price then also deciding on a high price will give a firm a payoff of 100, while going with a low price gives a better payoff of 150. And if the other firm goes with a low price then choosing a high price gives a payoff of -10, but selecting a low price in union gives a payoff of 0. Irrespective of what the other firm does the high price option is an inferior choice, and it is therefore a dominated strategy and can be ruled out.

## A dominated strategy

|  | | Firm 2 | |
|---|---|---|---|
|  | | High price | Low price |
| Firm 1 | High price | 100, 100 | 10, 150 |
|  | Low price | 150, -10 | 0, 0 |

Only the option of a low price remains, which is the dominant strategy for both firms. This reveals the Nash equilibrium of the game, the strategy where a player maximizes their payoffs given the strategy from the other player, which sees both firms deciding on low prices for payoffs of 0 each, or normal profits. But this result is worse than what the firms could have achieved if both had done the opposite and gone with high prices. That would have given them abnormal profits instead, and payoffs of 100 each. The duopoly game here is what's known as a prisoner's dilemma game, where participants would be better off working together and cooperating but individual incentives see them engage in self-destructive competition, as they attempt to win the approval of a third party for a higher payoff that's only available to one player.

In a one-off game the result in the duopoly game here may hold but if the game is repeated there may be another outcome, as players can then use a tit-for-tat strategy where they copy the other player's actions in the previous round of simultaneous choice. This may discourage lowering prices as two high price rounds (100 + 100 = 200) will dominate one round of undercutting and one round of the other firm setting a low price (150 + either 0 or -10). This could result in mutual high prices.

## *Battle of the Sexes Game*

It's not only firms who face games with their peers and consumers may face the same situation. The game below is a battle of the sexes game where a young couple are deciding between a sports game or a romantic comedy.

## Battle of the sexes game

|  | Her Sports | Romantic comedy |
|---|---|---|
| **Him** Sports | Best, Good | Worst, Worst |
| Romantic comedy | Worst, Worst | Good, Best |

As the most important thing for the young couple is to spend time together the worst option for both him and her is to be apart, with one at the sports game and the other watching the new romantic comedy on the big screen. The best result for him (first payoff of each pair) is for both to watch sports together, while her best outcome (second payoff of each pair) is for them to go to a romantic comedy. And the two of them both view doing what the other person likes best as a good outcome, but not their first choice. Yet a battle of the sexes scenario arises from their different ideal points and they can't both be achieved.

Unlike the last game there isn't a dominant and dominated strategy here, and when this occurs there are several possible solutions. One player could get the final say as the other acquiesces, or the players could choose to do both activities in turn with one now and the other next week (a mixed strategy). But if neither the man nor woman compromise for the short-term then one player may have to outmanoeuvre the other to get what they want.

A game tree can help participants reach a conclusion when stuck at a stalemate, and this sees the game turned from a situation where both players select their move simultaneously to one where each acts in turn. The following diagram allows the female half of the couple to think ahead to manipulate her boyfriend, looking at her own options after his choice to see what she needs to do, with S representing sports and RC the romantic comedy.

## Battle of the sexes sequential moves

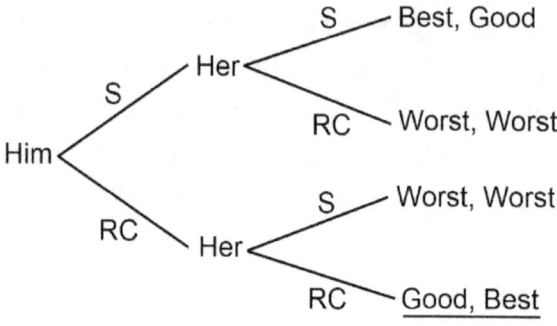

The diagram shows that the only way the woman can achieve her best option, underlined here, is if her boyfriend selects the romantic comedy first. Then she can select the same option and that's that. And this may come to pass if she uses what is known as a credible threat. If she went out and bought tickets to see the romantic comedy then it would be a waste of money for them not to see it (the threat), and her boyfriend may go along with her best option willingly, thus resolving the game.

The games used here show perfect information but in real life the payoffs may be unknown, particularly those possessed for the other player, games may be repeated for an unknown duration, or they may be zero-sum where one player can only gain if the other player loses. Putting these factors together can increase the uncertainty and fear in the game, and this may make it very difficult for those involved to develop an effective strategy.

www.ingramcontent.com/pod-product-compliance
Lightning Source LLC
Chambersburg PA
CBHW051726170526
45167CB00002B/825